Chapter 1: Getting Started

_____

Chapter 1.1 : Introduction to Meteorology

For thousands of years, human beings have been looking to the skies in an attempt to decipher the mysteries and patterns in weather. Unlike our ancestors, we today have a variety of instrumentation and tools which help us track and forecast weather. Today our techniques are more advanced in terms of technology and sophistication. This is evident in our use of satellite communication and imagery, as well as super computer modeling software which can render future trends every few hours. Given this level of advancement, you would think that forecasting the weather would be very easy to do and would require bare minimum knowledge on the subject. However, this is not true. I have compiled this book to help those who are coming into the field of meteorology for the first time to better understand the use and implementation of the tools available to weather forecasters, and to better familiarize themselves with applications commonly used in meteorology as a profession.

Understanding the history behind weather forecasting and how it has evolved over the past 100 years is very important to getting a grasp on the how's and why's of modern day forecasting techniques. Around 650 B.C. Babylonians attempted to predict short term variations and forecasts in the weather by observing cloud structure and appearance, as well as detecting halos which may signify

How to Use This Guide

The contents of this manual were written mainly to give the person reading it a basic understanding of how to prepare themselves for the world of meteorology. All of the information contained in this manual is factual and has been researched heavily to ensure the accuracy of the publication.

The first half of this guide will teach you how to set up your weather reporting area, and give you a good idea on how to acquire and store data used for producing your own forecasts, or sending data to the National Weather Service that is factual and accurate. The second half of this guide serves as a reference manual for those in the field. Sometimes we are in areas where our data connections will not give us access to Google. In these cases, this manual serves as a backup for quick reference on the go.

See you in the field!

Nick Szankovics
Webmaster, Weather-Talk.Net

Table of Contents

Chapter 1

Chapter 2

Chapter 3

Risks/Classification

Advisory Guide

Met Reference Guide

precipitation in the upper atmosphere. The Chinese took this a step further and created a calendar in 300 B.C. which separated the year into 24 festivals, each one signifying a different type of weather cycle. Early attempts at weather prediction were mostly based on a continuing cycle of weather that was believed to rarely deviate from one year to the next. Aristotle created a book known as *Meteorologica* , which was highly regarded as the top-most compendium on weather events for almost 2000 years. Written around 340 B.C . , this book contained theories on the formation of clouds, thunderstorms, hail, snow, lightning, and other weather phenomena. Although this book was highly regarded for almost 2000 years, it's theories were obliterated by the 17th century, as pioneers in the instrumentation process began to take fruition. Nicholas Cusa, a German scientist, developed the first hygrometer in the 1400's. This instrument was used to measure the humidity of air. Around 1592, Galileo Galilei constructed the first thermometer, which further advanced weather observations by allowing measurements of how warm or cold the surrounding air was. By 1643, Evangelista Torricelli had invented the barometer, which was vital in prediction of oncoming weather events. The observation of rising and falling pressure would indicate large scale storm systems days ahead of time.

With the development of these instruments, observations of weather data became possible. This allowed scientists to take samplings of data and record them, creating the first weather observatories. As this data became collected, the implementation of the telegraph in the mid-19th century allowed the sending of this data to distant stations hundreds, even a thousand miles away. This became the basis of the first large scale data network for transferring and deciphering weather data, as more observatories started popping up. As more of these stations became available, the data collected became more diversified from more locations, allowing the drawing of crude weather maps using the data plots. This became the birth of synoptic weather forecasting around the 1860's, when simultaneous observations from a large network of observing stations could be condensed into a forecast map based on pressure, precipitation, wind patterns, and temperatures. These early maps were no work of art, and required a lot of understanding of one's numerical terminology to decipher. However, they were effective as early indicators of a storm system, or period of calm that spawned the forecasting methods we now use today.

Even with this methodology of weather forecasting, the idea that nature gives signs of approaching events has been used for thousands of years by Native American Tribes,

African nations, and even the Mayans. Signs include the underside of a leaf being turned upwards to indicate rain or very humid conditions still holds true to this day. Other methods were not so steadfast, such as a halo around the moon that signifies oncoming snow. We know now that a halo does not represent a coming event, but is more of a phenomena than a weather observation. These methods are sometimes still used in less developed nations and Native American traditions.

Technology has advanced forecasting from a few drawn lines on a map, to global weather tracking and climate models. We now understand even more about our changing world, and that cycles usually can only last so long before they change. Mesoscale (local level) forecasting existed long before the tracking of large storms across entire continents. Up until the implementation of satellite data, the only way to track tropical weather was to receive reports from ships out at sea that would happen to stumble upon this weather. No other way of finding out if a hurricane was approaching existed at that point, and a "hurricane season" was unheard of up until the early 1950's. This should show our level of progress. However, for as much as we have traveled in the world of weather forecasting, we still have a long way to go in understanding weather events and forecasting even beyond the 2-3 day mark with relative certainty. The tools that have been developed over the last 2000 years have given us a way to steadily enhance our methods and apply them in new, and even more interesting, ways. Computer models have given us a good advancement over the last decade or so, as the age of computers descended upon us. It took a few more years after that for data to be readily available to whatever person wished to have such data. It also took a year or so after that for amateur meteorologists to come out of the woodwork and profess their love for the science without being ridiculed for not being a student of it.

It is apparent that if you have made it this far in your reading, that you are interested in the science as well, and chances are you were drawn to it by an event of some sort as you were growing up like I was. Whether it was a wind-storm, or a snowstorm that brought you here, your love for weather will take you a long way in absorbing the information contained in this book and applying it to either your studies, or hobby. Good luck to you in your journey through Meteorology, and it is my hopes that you learn something from this book or even use it to refresh yourself on the basics and some advanced applications.

This book is just the first in a line of many to teach aspiring meteorology buffs or professionals about the wonders of forecasting and understanding the weather. If you are like me you will walk away from this reading with a better understanding of meteorology, and you will use this book as a reference or field guide to help you on your way in your studies.

The study of weather will captivate until the end of time, with events and phenomena that will always show beauty in the natural world. Your interest in that is the first step in moving forward with your career aspirations. Welcome to the wonderful world of Meteorology!

Chapter 1.2 : Creating your Outline

Just like every journey, you need to be prepared to step out into the unknown. To do this you will need the proper tools to complete the journey safely and successfully. So what kind of tools do you need to study Meteorology? Below is a listing of instruments and devices you should have readily available to complete with this book.

- A pencil and a Pen.

- Writing Paper.

- A ruler (12 inches)

- A tape measure.

- A thermometer. (basic or digital)

- An anemometer. (measure wind speed)

- A computer with a spreadsheet program.

- A calculator. (can be on computer)

- A friend if possible.

- Proper clothing.

- An e-mail address. (required for reporting)

- A barometer. (Traditional or Digital)

After you have gathered the items listed above, you are now ready to begin your journey into Meteorology. The instrumentation listed above is easy to obtain, and can also be accessed with a home weather station if you have one. If you do not have these items, they can be purchased relatively cheaply online or in hardware stores.

Learning the devices involved in forecasting and how to apply them to your studies and data collection process is very important, as it serves as a basis for every forecast you produce. Incorrect use of these instruments can provide false data that doesn't help advance your skills nor produces forecasts that make any sense. Provided is a guide on how to use and read the instrumentation.

Thermometer: A basic tool for reading temperature. These can be traditional mercury based thermometers, or digital ones. the benefits to a digital thermometer is you can get easy readings below freezing temperatures, mercury ones have limitations sometimes that prevent them from accurately measuring below 10 degrees Fahrenheit. Using this device is simple, just place it in an area for 15-20 minutes and read the temperature on the display, or on the side of the glass tube.

Anemometer: This device is used in measuring wind speed and direction. Wind blows into a series of cups placed on a propeller swivel. The cups catch the wind and spin the propeller, calculating the speed at which the wind is blowing. The swivel aspect points the propeller in the direction in which the wind is blowing from, giving you the direction of the wind as well. Reading this instrument is simple, look at the display and read the numbers and direction from it. Try not to stand in an area where wind can funnel through, as this will make the winds appear faster than they actually are.

Barometer: This device is used to measure air pressure at your current elevation. Some barometers are digital, others are scale based. In both instances they are pretty similar in use, since you only need to look at the number displayed. High pressure is usually indicative of fair weather, while low pressure can indicate a storm. Air pressure can lower days before a storm, or can rise to indicate oncoming fair weather.

These are your tools for basic weather plots and forecasting. Weather stations will have other information like relative humidity and dew points. These options will be explored later on. Also be advised that an understanding of basic math will be needed to start meteorology, as a lot of calculations require an understanding of math fundamentals. Later examples will require a better understanding of physics and calculus, however we will cross that bridge when we arrive at it.

The better prepared you are for forecasting, the better your forecasts typically are. Rarely has a meteorologist who is properly prepared failed at their job. It is up to you to always keep the proper tools and methods accessible to yourself in order to create accurate weather data. Only then can you create the grids and maps needed to successfully implement your forecast.

Like any other task, preparation is key for starting a weather forecast. Creating an outline of the steps involved often times takes the guesswork out of it, and allows you to keep better track of what needs to be done and in what order. In this case, making an outline for a forecast is important before you start work on one. A nicely made outline will allow you to focus more on observations rather than remembering what to do.

This is where the writing paper, pencil, and pens come in handy. You can also use the wordpad or notepad on your personal computer or laptop to create the outline. It is important you include the following things in your outline to ensure you don't attempt to do too much at once.

---

1. Where are my observations taken? (City/State/Country)

2. What data do I wish to collect? (Temperature, Winds, Pressure, Dew points, Conditions)

3. How do I intend to collect this data? (Tools, Location)

4. At what time intervals? (1 hour, 3 hour, 6 hour, etc.)

5. Am I recording the data? (Spreadsheet, Paper, Graph)

6. Am I keeping the data? (Personal or Professional)

These are the first steps needed to compose an outline of your forecasting task. They establish why you are performing the observation, and also establish your local area dataset. This is important because throughout this book and throughout your journey through weather, this may be the primary area you focus on. So establishing your dataset early on makes it simple to replicate this outline for each task. This also holds true for daily reports as well.

Also be mindful that the data you collect should be stored for later, whether it be on a computer or on paper. If the data is stored via paper, make sure you have an area to file and store the information by a method that is precise and easy to reference. A file cabinet would work, with reports filed by date, for instance. Being able to reference the correct information quickly can often allow your forecasts to be completed more efficiently and with much more speed as compared to an unorganized data reference area.

You need to include other things in your outline as well. Taking the first steps to an outline may establish your demographic, however, it does not establish how you intend to compile and compose your data record.

1. Create a labeling system for your data records. You can use the date, or you can create an ID number such as WR-0001ABC. Either way you choose to label your data, ensure this formatting remains constant throughout your data records. Changing from one format to another can cause data to become jumbled or lost, or just plain confusing to reference.

2. Establish a spreadsheet or graph which contains all the necessary spots for the dataset you are collecting. Lines paper can work well for this, and use the ruler to draw vertical lines to separate data fields.

3. Ensure the heading labels on your fields remain the same over the entire course of data collection. Nothing is more confusing than attempting to reference a specific piece of data and having it in a different place 5 pages in.

4. If collecting Snowfall totals, ensure that you use multiple rulers and yardsticks positioned in a remote or low traffic area to allow for the best measurement success.

5. Position your weather data collection site in the same area that you place these rules and yardsticks to allow for a

uniform collection area from the same site.

6. Make sure the battery on your laptop or tablet device is fully charged before venturing out to your site. Chances are, it will not have an electrical outlet for charging, and some of these devices do not have chargers included with them for your vehicle.

7. Make sure you have the proper clothing on for your collection site. If it will be cold, wear layers of clothing and a winter hat, scarf, and insulated gloves. Be aware that the same weather conditions you are attempting to record are also affecting you, so be ready for it.

8. Bring water with you in your vehicle or on your persons. Data collection sometimes takes a while to conduct, so staying hydrated is very important. This is especially true in very cold and dry conditions, as well as summer months when it can be hot and humid.

9. Bring a snow shovel if it's snowing. This is an often forgotten step on an outline that can cause big problems. Often times, your vehicle will get stuck in an area while it's snowing out and you are taking observational data. Bring a shovel to clear a pathway for your vehicle to exit

the site, as these observation sites are remote and do not have regular traffic. This makes it difficult for passer-bys to know that you are stuck.

10.   Bring something to eat. If you are on a site all day, you are going to get hungry and fatigued. The best way to combat this is to bring something to eat that has proteins and good carbohydrates. Do not bring candy or soda which has high sugar, but empty calories. This can actually hurt you more than it helps by not allowing your body to recharge the energy it needs.

11.   Bring a first aid kit. Sometimes while you are out in the field, something may cut you or hurt you, so having a first aid kit comes in handy in preventing infection, or bleeding injuries.

12.   Have a cell phone. Be prepared to dial 911 in an emergency, or report a very hazardous weather condition, such as a tornado. This is a life saver, and since most cell phones now have GPS technology, they will be able to find your location if you have no idea where you are.

13.   If possible, have a weather radio with you with a fresh set of batteries.

Some conditions may cause you to remain in your location, while others may cause you to have to leave immediately. Monitor the weather radio for these conditions.

14.   Always notify someone else to where you are going to. If for some reason you become stuck or cannot exit the area, having notified someone else where you are will help aid in emergency services locating you and helping you if something should happen.

This outline should allow you to be ready to begin your data collection process. Reviewed below in quick format as follows:

- Create Data Label System

- Create a spreadsheet/Grid

- Label Table Headers Correctly

- Place Yardsticks/rulers in Multiple Spots

- Establish a permanent Collection area

- Make Sure Laptop/Tablet Batteries are Charged

- Bring Correct Clothing for Conditions

- Bring Water to drink

- Bring Snow Shovel (if possible snow)

- Bring real food

- Bring First Aid kit

- Have a Cell Phone (Charged)

- Bring Weather Radio (Charged)

- Notify friend/neighbor where I am going

It is also a good idea to bring with you a flashlight with charged batteries just in case you have to maneuver around in low light conditions or at night. Make sure the lumens on the flashlight are bright enough to see in the area you are in, or to signal someone if you have to. Once you have completed this part of the outline, you can move on to the data collection part of the outline.

---

1. Use instrument to read data located on your spreadsheet.

---

2. Enter the value observed as well as correct date and time.

3. Recheck value once again versus instrumentation.

4. If correct, repeat this step for additional fields.

Continue this process until all fields required on your data sheet have been completed. To ensure accuracy, you can repeat the entire data set once again, however, a recheck after each observation will ensure you have the correct value to input or write into your data field.

This is a full outline of how to correctly record and observe weather data while keeping yourself organized and safe. Keeping a record of your outline with you will always ensure that you are prepared for the worst when visiting your data collection site.

Date	Time	Temp	W/Spd	W/Dir	DewPt
2/2/13	0030	12	5 mph	N	10
2/2/13	0100	10	3 mph	N	10
2/2/13	0130	10	2 mph	N	10

2/2/13	0200	11	1 mph	NE	10
2/2/13	0230	12	4 mph	N	11
2/2/13	0300	12	5 mph	NE	12
2/2/13	0330	11	6 mph	N	11

As you can see the information is readily accessible and in an easy-to-read format. However you use this information is up to you, and what observations you make are completely up to you as well. After all, you are the potential forecaster. A rule of thumb is to collect as much information and data as you can from your site, that way you do not have to skip any important forecast details such as heat index, wind chill, and dry air.

Keeping records consistent and accurate is the best way to sharpen your forecasting skills. Using things like "garbage" data, which is essentially data not collected correctly or has no bearing on your forecasting plan, can often jumble up the input process and take away precious minutes or even hours from a successful forecast.

Chapter 1.3 : Applying a Method

Creating your own method of acquiring data and samples is a very important aspect of your learning process. Sticking to the same way of doing things, hence a routine, can often times save you a lot of trouble when discrepancies start to emerge in data. Much like a scientific method, your routine should adhere to acquiring and collecting your data from the same sources and same areas, as to prevent contamination or corruption.

An example of corruption of data is to collect the information from a source in the same general area, but several thousand feet higher in elevation. Elevation plays a huge role in the conditions experienced from area to area, so acquiring data for a valley city from a mountain town isn't going to pan out very well on your results sheet. Sticking to the same areas will guarantee that your readings will be accurate and consistent, and not contain the wrong data to compose your forecast with.

This method of what is known as "microcasting" often takes place in states that contain an ocean coastline. A state like Florida will often have two separate forecasts for the same city, simply because it has an ocean coastline that will influence that weather pattern in that small area in some way. Forecasters will refer to these as Shore and Inland forecasts, which can differ greatly from each other, even given a few miles. This method is done because shoreline communities who would adhere to the inland forecast might experience something totally different.

Methods also exist in the act of forecasting. Large events that are unpredictable and require more time to test and acquire information for are usually put into a method called "downplay". This method is often used on tv or media outlets to defer the possible effects of an impending weather event until a strong consensus is reached on the probabilities of such an event. This method is not used to confuse or to misdirect the listener or viewer, it is used to inform the person of the possibility of the event and that the forecaster needs better clarity on the forecast period. This type of method occurs 3-5 days before an event, and usually involves some kind of confusion in the computer model data.

Another method is called "hyping" a storm or event. This method usually occurs when a forecaster believes that his or her forecast is on target for a large event occurring in a 80-100% probability margin. A lot of professionals prefer to shy away from this method because it creates panic and disinformation within the

public concerning a weather event. Needless
hysteria and panic can cost lives and the
safety of others, so responsibility is needed
to be reserved when approaching an event using
such a method. Sometimes, this method is
inevitable for large storm systems like
hurricanes and nor'easters. These events are
very large scale and often have large impacts
on areas even outside of the forecast cones.
Resorting to this method does not make you a
bad forecaster, but it does require much more
confidence in a forecast than just staring at a
computer model and hoping it does what you want
it to do over the course of its next few runs.

You can also play the middle-ground
method, which essentially allows you to take
either side of the equation and run with it.
However, this is often just as dangerous
because it shows your lack of interpretation
and understanding of a particular situation. At
the same time it could just mean that you are
waiting on a more viable solution from a run of
computer models or data set. So, despite
sounding like you are trying to skate the fence
between the two options, you really are just
weighing the ideas back and forth to a more
logical conclusion.

No matter what method you decide to take
into your skill-set, it is always important to
remember that with every forecast your produce
there will be many people skeptical about the
outcome of it. This derives from botched

forecast periods and inconclusive data concerning large events of the past, and nothing to do with you however. So learn to understand that you may have to deal with people telling you are wro9ng very often, even though you have done your best to put together a forecast that is well-informed and supported. You will have people trying to persuade you towards one method or the other. Just be warned that whatever road you take on this path, you will have to be prepared to answer for your inconsistencies should something wrong arise. Every forecaster has been wrong at some point in their career, so your failures should be your fuel for success.

Creating your own method is fairly simple. However, you will need to write down what it is you do to formulate your data in order to adhere to that rubric through every aspect of your formulation. Always take a minute to stop your work and figure out how close you are sticking to your method. Often times a simple misstep can cause a forecast to become completely unusable. Because of this, keeping track of how you are processing your data, and taking a few breaks to clear your mind and relax can remove those chances of becoming too lost in your work. Getting lost in your work often leads to errors that become difficult to spot until the entire project is completed. Not causing these problems first will always save time from your day.

Part of a method is also creating a way to present your forecast to the public, or even to yourself. Sometimes presentation is about graphics and fancy gadgets, other times it may be a simple note or set of notes given to your audience. Presentation is about putting the large amount of data you collect into an easily understood format. If your forecast is for an audience, you have to assume that a majority of your audience will not know specific weather terminology or abbreviations. Because of this, you will need to simplify the presentation. Often times aspiring TV meteorologists will present their forecasts to others in their family or friends. When doing this always assume that no one in your audience has a clue what you are talking about. However, refrain from watering down the language to the point of sounding condescending. You are not trying to insult your audience's intelligence, you are trying to inform them in an easy to digest format. Adapt your method based on the results you hear from your friends and family. Often times this type of audience is more forgiving than an actual audience, and will help you figure out how to fine tune your delivery and presentation before expending your reach.

By following these disciplines you can successfully create a forecasting plan that fits your needs. Being unique in the business is a strong selling point. No one likes the same old boring weatherman, so your personality and unique method will attract new fans and professionals that will be willing to work with you. Hence, a method is very important to both your early learning days and your late connections game.

Chapter 2: The Elements

Chapter 2.1 : The Water Cycle

The origins of weather on Earth can be simplified down to a single cycle. This is called "The Water Cycle". This is the method in which water vapor arrives into the atmosphere, creates weather, and eventually comes back down to Earth. Several components exist within this cycle that should be noted.

The Sun: Heat and exposure from the sun creates energy in which   causes liquid water to evaporate, or become vapor. It also heats water in the lakes and oceans that create currents that allow areas to evaporate more than others. These currents often run north and south of the Equator and can be seen quite easily on water temperature charts. The sun is constantly there, so even on cloudy days, it will still be sending solar radiation to Earth, causing evaporation.

Terrain: The terrain elements of a particular area can often dictate how fast or how slow the transition from water to water vapor then back to water occurs. Examples of this are mountains and valleys. Typically vapor being forced up over a large mountain will cause it to condense into water/snow much quicker on the upslope side, and leaving it relatively dry on the downslope side. Valleys can often channel winds and different ways that may lead to quicker evaporation.

Size of Water Source: Smaller water sources such as smaller rivers and streams often do not aid much in the water cycle process, as they often do not contribute much to the overall saturation at upper levels. However, oceans, larger rivers, and larger lakes can create their own weather patterns because they have more water to work with and can often localize the water cycle over its own area.

Aside from these factors, the water cycle is a pretty easy concept to visualize and understand. It has remained this way for millions of years, and does not intend to change for millions of years more. The following is a quick synopsis of what comprises the water cycle:

---

1. Water from a source evaporates, rising upwards since it is lighter than the air around it.

2. The water vapor reaches the troposphere, condensing against particles of dust/dirt blown by wind into the atmosphere. The cold air sublimates (causes it to go from vapor to solid) by crystalizing it. The

crystals move around once another and concentrate, forming clouds.

3. More and more crystals build up, forcing the weight of the cloud to begin to overcome the buoyancy of the air around it. The crystals begin to fall towards the ground.

4. The ground collects the water and funnels it into rivers, lakes, and oceans.

5. The process starts all over again.

This basic process is what fuels weather and all of its components. If this did not occur, we would not have weather systems on the planet, and life would die out due to stagnation and lack of oxygen. Trees require water to grow and produce oxygen for life on this planet. Without the water cycle, there would be no water, hence no life.

Understanding the properties and movements of water is the foundation of meteorology. Without this general understanding, forecasters could not do their work and compose forecasts in an accurate way. Since air moves much the same as water, we can deduce from that idea that the flow and dispersion of air reacts much in the same way as water does, but on a less dense scale.

Knowing what is involved in the water cycle can also help you spot formation areas of weather events. Often times, sea breezes can be prime locations for weather development in particular areas. Knowing where to look and how these conditions relate with the cycle itself will help identify the mechanics that drive these events.

Just like water, packets of air will break apart to move around obstructions, even if that obstruction is opposing water. The swirls created in the wake of these opposing forces can often create mesoscale(localized) areas of adverse or calm weather conditions. The results depend on how violently those forces collide or how gently. Often times the forces can create larger areas of weather which move around the swirls created by the obstruction. So, much in the way that water works, the air works in a much similar way. Also, as different temperatures factor into the surrounding air, you create channels, or pathways, for similar pockets of air to move through. These create steering currents for this air to interact with, much like streams of warmer water moving through colder water. These are often independent of a larger flow pattern and need to be factored in. So by studying the flow of water, you can typically form ideas about the flow of air in typical weather patterns. Experimenting with the dynamics of water is often the fastest way to understand the dynamics and movements of air patterns, and can often lead to a concrete way to study the movements of weather patterns without actually being there to watch them.

To get a better idea of how this is done, use a flat pan of water and use various methods to make the water move. Now toss in objects to impede the movement and see how the water reacts in the pan. Jot down notes upon each experiment and note down the differences that occur with different types of objects. Make sure to use a flat pan, as a rounded bowl will not adhere to the same set of mechanics as a pan will, plus you can apply terrain to the bottom of the flat pan to add to the further study of fluid motion. Performing these physical studies will often allow you to get a better idea of how the process works as a whole, and prevent you from misunderstanding the situations that may arise from learning fluid mechanics.

Chapter 2.2 : Applied Formation of Clouds

This section covers the formation of clouds. Clouds, by nature, are suspended ice crystals that have formed around pieces of pollution in the atmosphere. This pollution can be man-made from carbon emissions, or from naturally occurring pollution that has blown into the troposphere. These can include sand, dust, and smoke from fires/volcanoes. Ice crystals form around this debris and form the clouds that we see. The crystals reflect all colors of the prism, which make them look white in appearance. However, too many crystals packed into a confined area will start to block out the light at lower levels. This makes the clouds appear ominous, or dark in appearance.

Clouds can form pretty much at any point between ground level and the upper troposphere. These layers are often determined by level of moisture involved, upper air conditions, and temperature contrasts at the resulting layers. Winds in the atmosphere also have a bit to do with the types of clouds that are seen during formation. Let's take a look at different cloud types and what normally causes them to form.

Cumulus: These are the billowy, puffy-type clouds you will find associated with both fair and bad weather. Often times these types of clouds can signal lighter winds aloft which allow them to possibly continue their upwards ascent.

Stratus: These are layered cloud formations that can signal abundant moisture in the atmosphere. These also signal that there is a flattening wind dynamic in the lower troposphere which spread these clouds out over a wide area.

Cirrus: These are clouds that form in the upper troposphere and on the cusp of the stratosphere. These clouds are whispy in appearance and get their feathered look from strong upper level wind dynamics that pull these formations into a sheared look. These types of clouds can often signal a warm from many hours ahead of time.

Fog: Fog is typically considered a cloud even though it is more of a phenomenon than an actual cloud. Fog occurs when dew points at the surface combined with light steering currents allow suspended water particles to remain trapped at the surface. Normally the fuel for fog would be a water source that has its evaporation slowed by stagnant dew points and an accelerated evaporation dynamic. Fog is often burned off by the sunshine or lifts into higher levels of the troposphere to form different types of clouds.

There are many other variations of these types of clouds listed above, and can all occur at the same time. Learning to identify these types of clouds can help you determine the forecast simply by looking to the sky. Thunderstorms contain pretty much every cloud type, and occupy much more space in the air than typical versions of the clouds mentioned above. Cumulonimbus is the term used for a thunderstorm because thunderstorms derive from cumulus clouds that have accelerated updraft and allows the cloud to build upwards towards the stratosphere. Try watching a thunderstorm build during the day and see if you can recognize the different types of clouds contained within it.

There are also special types of clouds that are associated with phenomena in the weather world. Listed below is some of those special types of clouds and how they form.

- **Shelf Cloud:** These types of clouds are found on the leading edge of thunderstorms and are formed from outflow winds from the storm. Typically these clouds lead the storm, but contain winds forcing away from the storm. Think of these clouds as being the snow billowing up on the end of your snow shovel. As you push the snow away, it builds up on the edge of the shovel.

- **Wall Cloud:** These clouds are contained in supercell thunderstorms, where the updraft is at its greatest and the inflow winds meet the updraft. These areas can rotate independently from the storm, or not rotate at all. Often times these wall clouds can indicate mesocyclonic development and tornadoes. Not all wall clouds produce tornadoes, but they all do have the capability of doing so. Storm chasers often look for a wall cloud to identify which storm has a higher risk for development a tornado.

- **Scud Cloud:** Scud clouds are typically formed during thunderstorm and indicate that there is very moist air rapidly moving into the storm. They will appear like smoke rising from the landscape and merge with the overrunning storm above them. It is an important fact to remember that scud clouds are NOT tornadoes.

- **Roll Clouds:** These clouds are formed often when a series of cumulus clouds crosses over a body of water and are overtaken by a strong midlevel wind. This actually allows the clouds to rotate on its side. This does not indicate severe weather, but it does indicate strong midlevel winds aloft.

- **Lenticular Clouds**: These clouds appear on top of large mountain rangers and appear to be like layers of pancakes draped over the mountain top. These clouds form when pockets of moist and cool air gets trapped between pockets of warmer air. These temperature contrasts and moisture differences leaves gaps in the cloud development area, making these clouds seem to be stacked or floating atop one another.

Understanding these different types of clouds can often help you in figuring out your forecasts. Stormy weather usually requires a specific set of conditions in order to remain stormy. Knowing to identify these clouds can let you know whether the existence of those conditions are occurring or not. It is important to remember that all clouds are made from the same materials.

Chapter 2.3 : Wind and Movement

Wind and movement is a very important factor in meteorology and forecasting, as it allows us to take a good guess at conditions which may exist or develop ion a particular area. Without wind or movement, we would not have to forecast much. This would be due to the fact that conditions in certain areas would never change and the storms would not move.

Wind is caused by the difference in temperatures at all layers of the atmosphere. Because the sun does not heat things evenly, air will rise and fall based on their relative temperature to one another. This creates movement and allows wind to occur. Friction with land or water has different effects on these air parcels, which allow them to speed up or slow down dependent on the surrounding temperature differences. Also, changes in wind speed can also be caused by barometric differences in air pressure. This could cause channels to be condensed between resulting equal lines of barometric pressure (isobars) and cause the air to speed up as if pushed upon by a force.

Wind movement and speed is not the only important aspect of weather forecasting.

Direction is also as important, as it can tell you as the forecaster where the elements are coming from in the forecast, as well as telling you where the temperature flow is resulting from. Typically in the United States and Canada, a southerly flow can result in warmer and more humid conditions. A Northerly flow could result in a colder and drier weather pattern. Because of this, wind direction is important and vital to the success of a forecast.

Because all of these patterns are ever changing with constantly changing temperatures, the winds are always changing as well. Movement of weather patterns and storms is often dictated by this, and frontal ranges are almost always guided by the differences in both temperatures and wind direction. These two aspects share a constant symbiosis with one another to help fuel the pattern. In forecasting, you are always looking for where the sources of weather are deriving from, allowing you to better analyze what behaviors those parcels of air are going to take.

Because air/wind reacts much the same way that water does when encountering opposing forces and obstacles, we can study what air typically does in a particular situation by putting water into the same set of conditions and watching the reactions that take place. This is known as "Fluid mechanics", and since air acts like water, the same principles tend to apply. Cold air sinks while warm air rises, the same as if you place warm and cold water into a bowl. The cold water will settle to the bottom and the warmer, less dense water will collect at the surface. This is the same way that air within frontal movements occurs. The less dense warm air is forced up and over the dome of more dense cold air and the resulting force causes weather to occur. So it is important to remember that the conditions for some powerful weather may exist in some areas, however, a trigger is required to cause that weather to ignite. This usually occurs when the wind pattern shifts and generates those conditions for the parcels of air at the surface, forcing them up and over the dome and causing them to condense very quickly. This mechanism will be explored further inside this manual.

Measuring wind speed is relative. This means that the speeds may different from area to area due to landscape, elevation, or even specific weather anomalies. When measuring wind speed it is always important to remember that you should take an average of all measurements recorded over the course of a full minute. Take into account the average of the direction as well, as wind has a tendency to swirl and do particular mechanics on a microscale, even though the larger direction of the wind remains constant. If you are going to take a measurement of the wind, ensure that you are in an open area free of excess obstructions and landscape (trees, overlooming hills, etc.) and ensure your body isn't blocking the direction of the wind. Take several measurements over the course of one minute with an anemometer. Record your speeds and average them together using the number of samples (If you take 5 readings, add together all 5 readings, then divide by 5.) and you will have your average for the wind speed. In terms of direction, you look at the direct the wind was coming in and count the directions. An example would be 5 readings: North, north-east, north, north-northeast, north. Considering 3 of the 5 observations are from the north, you can essentially deduce that the dominant wind direction is from the north. Essentially your reading will look something like this:

Time/ Wind Speed @ 220 pm	Direction of Wind
10sec 12 mph	North (1)
20sec 14 mph	North-East (1)
30sec 13 mph	North (2)
40sec 12 mph	North-northeast (1)
50sec 10 mph	North (3)
Average Speed: 12.2 MPH	Average Direction: North

Normally this is a wonderful way to keep track of wind speeds over the course of a forecasting or observing period. Winds will fluctuate, but giving an average is usually the best way to convey the idea of how the winds are reacting outside. Sometimes inside of these one minute spans, you may get wind gusts. A wind gust is defined by winds that typically exceed the average wind by 10-15 mph minimum. Since gusts can occur at any time during these periods, if your recording session in the one minute contains a gust, note this down as well, but do not apply it to averages. As such:

Time/ Wind Speed @ 220 pm	Direction of Wind
10sec 12 mph	North
20sec 35 mph	Northeast
30sec 13 mph	North
40sec 12 mph	North
50sec 11 mph	Northeast
Average Wind Speed: 12 mph	Average Wind Direction: North
Gust: 35 mph NE @ 14:20:20 EDT	

The difference here is the average is based off of 4 readings instead of 5 readings, that way the ambient wind speed that is normal during that time period remains unadjusted to the higher number. Only do this when recording winds to report, and only do it if the gusts are not very frequent. Frequent wind gusts can be a sign that the wind is changing and increasing in speed over all. This is just a small guide to go by, as you can choose to record wind speeds any way you would like, however, the standard for doing so it typically the best way to get accurate results.

There are other units of measurement for wind other than Miles per hour (mph). These are typically used by forecast offices to determine both international and technical data that does not conform to the American unit of measurement. Below are a few commonly used units of wind speed measurement:

Knot - This unit of measurement is equal to one nautical mile per hour (1.852 km) or 1.151 mph. Derived from counting the number of knots that unspooled from the reel of a chip log in a specific amount of time. Commonly used in maritime reporting of conditions and coastal observations.

Kilometer - A kilometer is smaller than a mile, but it's bit over half the distance. A kilometer is roughly .621371192237334 Miles. Rounded down, we get .62 miles per Kilometer. This is typically why KM readings seem double that of MPH readings. It is also based of the metric system which is typically a more accurate way of measuring conditions.

Gale – Although there are varying definitions of what defines a "Gale", this is a strong wind that typically remains sustained between 39-54 mph according to the National Weather Service.

Storm – This wind measurement typically refers to when sea surface winds in a given area are expected to become sustained greater than 54 mph. These types of measurements used to be used to describe tropical cyclone conditions before tropical storm warnings and hurricane warnings were put into use. Now this uniot normally refers to very strong areas of low pressure that generate strong wind fields at sea.

       To classify the ranges of winds that may be experienced, the Beaufort Windforce Scale was created to give people an idea of what could be experienced on a given day. We have provided the entire scale to help you better understand how these conditions are derived, and how to apply that to your meteorological work.

Value	Description
0	Calm
1	Light Air
2	Light Breeze
3	Gentle Breeze
4	Moderate Breeze
5	Fresh Breeze
6	Strong Breeze
7	Moderate Gale (32-38 mph)
8	Fresh Gale (39-46 mph)
9	Strong Gale (47-54 mph)
10	Storm/Whole Gale (55-63 mph)
11	Violent Storm (64-74 mph)
12	Hurricane (>74 mph)

The scale above references hurricane as being on the scale, however, this only references the force of the wind involved. That is why as of 2013-2104, the National Weather Service adopted Hurricane Force Wind Warnings, to help better identify the difference between the two. This policy and standard was adopted out of the confusion surrounding SuperStorm Sandy, which (according to the national Weather Service) had turned subtropical before making landfall in New Jersey. Despite this subtropical characteristic, the storm ravaged the area with category 2 hurricane force winds and battered areas all up and down the east coast of the United States.

It is also important to note that wind does have density, and the colder the wind is, the more dense it will be. This is why colder wind may feel stronger against objects or the body than a warm wind of the same speed. Damage on standing objects like homes and erected structures will be more likely in a cold wind scenario than a warm wind situation. Most of the damage that occurs in warmer wind below hurricane force happens concerning trees that still have leaves and surface area on them. This added area allows the wind to have a better surface to hit against, thus allowing more force to occur. This is why stronger winds during the winter usually don't knock down trees, because the surface area for the wind to hit has been greatly reduced because of no foliage.

Determining wind speed and direction can often be a very important part of your forecast or day, as it precludes all other events which will occur during that day. Wind allows steering, mixing, and movement of the air, so watching it closely can often let you know hours in advance if inclement weather may be approaching or not. More information about wind dynamics will be covered in later areas.

Chapter 2.4 : Air Convergence

The convergence or mixing of air is what weather is all about. Frontal boundaries and these types of mixing air dynamics drive most of the weather on Earth. Learning how these types of dynamics occur and react is very important to determining how your forecast will pan out.

Frontal boundaries are one of the more common areas of air convergence, and typically trigger most of the volatile weather we experience here on Earth. There are several different types of frontal boundaries:

Cold Front: Cold fronts occur when cold air pushes against warmer air ahead of it, forcing it upwards above the dome of cold air. This violent lift causes quick and severe weather in many cases, with thunderstorms being very common along the fringes of this type of front.

Warm Front: A warm front occurs when warmer air progresses forwards behind an area of colder air. Since warm air cannot manipulate the denser cold air in front of it, it moves at the speed of the retreating cold air. The warm air runs up and over the colder air, but not as violently as in a cold front. This typically provides a more dreary and rainy type day with minimal uplifting.

Occluded Front: This type of frontal boundary occurs when an area of colder air stalls and causes both areas of cold and warm air to become somewhat equal in their areas. Minimal lifting occurs along these areas, but a more stagnant type of precipitation can occur along these areas due to minimal movement.

These frontal boundaries are normally associated with areas of low or high pressure, and normally follow the paths of those features pretty closely. Watching what areas these features develop along low pressure areas can give a good idea where stronger or more violent weather will occur. Since the type of front usually follows the type of air associated with it, warm fronts typically develop along the eastern side of a low pressure system, while cold fronts develop along the western side of the same system. This is often due in part to the wind direction and circulation around the area of low pressure itself (counter-clockwise).

Frontal boundaries do not always signal bad weather. Other dynamics are usually required to trigger storms and rain along these areas, however, the presence of mixing air is often a conducive environment to get this type of weather to foster. However, you will often notice these areas of weather confined to the frontal areas where the dynamics are most ripe for development.

The easiest way to mimic the dynamics of a cold front is to cool down a bottle of water in a refrigerator. Take that beverage out of the fridge and introduce it to a warmer area of air like your ambient air in a room. You will shortly begin to see water forming along the outside of the beverage, even if you have not opened it. This is because the moisture in the warmer air is condensing against the colder object in the room, much like clouds form. The colder object represents the focal point of airmass temperature change, thus causes weather (condensation).

Dynamics in the atmosphere are very similar to this process. It works the same way for all types of weather, where water condenses against the colder airmass from the warmer area of air. The way and how violent it falls back to the ground has a lot more to do with how accelerated the mechanics are in the atmosphere to produce the process. This is why sometimes during the winter a much colder air mass can cause much lighter snow, even though its fuel source is warm and moisture-filled. The colder air holds much less water content, therefore, when condensing the water, it dries up some of that fuel and fails to produce a heavier snowfall.

Another common occurrence happens in Florida pretty regularly. It is called a "seabreeze", and it is an area of cooler air from off the ocean that collides with the warmer and more humid air over the mainland. This causes the warm air to force upwards quickly and develop some thunderstorms and rain. This is the dynamics of a cold front at work on a smaller scale, with the breeze itself serving as the colder air to the front, and the warmer air adding the fuel to the storms as it is forced up and over the cooler air. The same kind of common dynamic occurs with a cold front along a low pressure area. Once the cooler air arrives, the instability is replaced with a more stable air mass.

So why do some weather events take place without a defined frontal boundary? Despite the non-existence of a boundary, air still mixes pretty well on its own. Warm air rises and cooler air sinks, constantly mixing the air. The faster this process occurs, the more volatile the interaction becomes and forms clouds. These clouds continue to build over the area of faster mixing and can often build into thunderstorms. This occurrence is common during springtime and summertime situations where the hot sun allows the lower levels of the troposphere to warm and colder air from aloft mixes down as the warm air rises. In essence it will form its own area of instability and allow that disturbance to continue until the elements of rapid mixing is removed. A quick thunderstorm can serve to balance the air mass and stabilize the area around it. We call these "pop-up" storms, because they seem to bubble up from out of almost nowhere. The potential for these types of storms is often predicted using a set of indicators that will often tell how unstable the resulting air mass is. This does not always mean the entire area of unstable air will produce weather, but it does give an indication of the potential for it to do so.

The values and indicators that often put the potential for these air masses to produce inclement weather are studied closely, especially by the Storm Prediction Center (SPC) because they often serve as the same indicators for the possibility of tornadoes and other severe weather in the nation. Below is a listing of factors used in determining the instability of a resulting air mass:

CAPE (Convective Available Potential Energy): This value is used to measure the total available convective energy potential for a specific area. This is measured in Joules per kilogram, which is an energy indicator. The higher the cape value, the more likely a thunderstorm will be able to form in that area. However, you can still fail to have a thunderstorm even with a large cape value simply because they are other factors that determine how that cape is used. Below is a quick indicator chart for CAPE values:

CAPE Value (J/kg)	Definition
0001-1000	Marginally Unstable
1000-2500	Moderately Unstable
2500-3500	Very Unstable
3500+	Extremely Unstable

There are also other type of CAPE values that are included with this definition. The most common are MUCAPE and MLCAPE. MUCAPE means Most Unstable CAPE, and is calculated by looking into the bottom 300mb of a CAPE parcel and finding the most unstable value contained. This often helps out a bit with locating the chances for tornadoes and strong winds. MLCAPE is mean layer CAPE which is used in the lowest 100 mb of a parcel of air to find the mean value among that particular parcel. Often good to find where more probabilistic areas of development can occur.

CAPE is also typically used to calculate the maximum potential speed of updraft within a parcel of air. This can be found by using the equation: MPU = Sqrt(2*CAPE) , which will give you the maximum potential updraft speed in that parcel of air. This will help locate area where updrafts may break other barriers holding development at bay.

CAP (Capping Inversion): This is a layer of warm air aloft, typically a few thousand feet above the ground that serves to suppress cloud development above a certain height. The air parcels rising into this area tend to become cooler than the surrounding air, which allows them to sink back down towards the ground. Because of this, air cannot overcome this capping area until rising air becomes powerful enough to "break the cap" Once this occurs though, thunderstorms will be allowed to form. The CAP often will be in place when large CAPE values exist, and the cap must be broken in order for that large energy potential to be released high enough into the atmosphere to produce thunderstorms.

Marine Layer: For those of us who live along the shoreline or close to an ocean, we experience something called a marine layer. This is typically an area of cooler air that is not as moist as the surrounding air. This tends to dry out its layer of the troposphere and inhibit the development of storms or rain in that area by removing the instability. Typically a marine layer will exist once the wind direction is coming from off the ocean, and allowing the stable and drier air to make its way inland. This layer can also serve to break apart developing thunderstorms by embedding itself into the mid layers of the developing storms and depriving them of their fuel and updraft.

So as you can see, other types of mixing concerning air have a lot to do with the process of weather. Knowing these factors can often help keep you from incorrectly producing a forecast, and allow your target audience to remain properly informed of any storms in their future.

Chapter 2.5: Air Pressure

Air pressure is a very important thing to be analyzing during your weather forecasts. Often times, the air pressure outside will dictate how the weather for the day will be going, and whether or not there are problems on your horizon.

Something to look for when recording the air pressure outside is if the pressure has been rising or falling during the course of a recording period. Falling air pressure can signal the onset of a low pressure system, which makes it more likely that storms and rain may be on the way. A rising barometer can signal the end of stormy weather or the onset of fair weather. Storms typically do not form under higher air pressure because it puts a limit on the heights of the cloud formations that derive from it. So paying attention to the barometer and checking it every hour or so will help you in your forecast.

Low air pressure is typically responsible for the onset of large storms because cloud formations and organization of those clouds are less inhibited under less pressure. They are allowed to grow into large formations, like thunderstorms, and produce more violent weather. This also means that the air is less stabilized and that "bubbles" of lower pressure can allow the rise of warmer air quicker into the lower atmosphere, which allows rain and storms to be almost inevitable. By watching how the pressure rises and falls you can form a pattern in which you can track centers of high and low pressure and how they correlate to the weather that precedes them.

The differences in air pressure are one of the more defining features for storm steering there is. Large areas of low pressure will spin counter-clockwise and draw storms and moisture towards their centers. Almost like a bathtub drain that draws the water in from the tub and circles around the lower pressure. High pressure will spin clockwise and serve to repel storms and clouds, which is why most high pressure days are sunny and dry. Around these areas of differing pressure, we look for a more important feature that tells us a lot about wind and storm flow. These features are called "Isobars".

Isobars are lines of equal pressure that are drawn on a forecast map. They cannot be physically seen within the storms or on a satellite image. But these lines of equal pressure can cause a lot of weather. The closer the isobars are together, the more pressure change over a smaller area there is. This usually means that the center of lowest or highest pressure is strengthening or becoming pushed up against an opposing pressure force. This causes wind between those isobars, as it acts much like taking a balloon and squeezing it down will one end open. The air will rush through a narrower channel and become stronger. Peoples who live in cities experience this very often, when a small bit of wind is forced between two buildings and the resulting wind is much stronger than the original. The same holds true for an area of water forced out of a smaller opening. The result is a much more forceful and faster moving water stream.

The result of this wind can exist in the lower levels (surface) or the upper levels of an area of weather. Normally rain has a sinking effect on the air around it, cooling it so it falls towards to the ground. This is why sometimes storms can rain themselves out, which means they become so cool that they can no longer sustain their updrafts and then fall apart. But it can also cool the rush of air in the upper levels, allowing it to sink towards the ground and affect people and cities. Because of this, it is important to note isobars and areas of weather which happen to be around those isobars. This is why sometimes a calm day can turn into a very windy day that damages homes and trees.

Also, the natural cooling effect of the atmosphere can transfer this wind to ground level as well, which is why it is important to monitor the current temperature projections around areas with compact isobars. A cool atmosphere will push things towards the ground, and that includes winds. This often happens during the autumn months when cooler air remains aloft while slightly warmer air remains at the surface. As the air cools more it forces wind down to the surface which results in a fair day, but very windy. It's very important to know the way this dynamic works so that you can fine-tune your forecasts based on the presence of these dynamics in the atmosphere.

Air pressure can also be dictated by temperature contrasts. Warm air can hold moisture and rise, lowering the air pressure around it. Cold air is dry and sinks, raising the air pressure around it. This means that high pressure is typically a colder air than that of lower pressure, which would explain why low pressure areas hold moisture whereas high pressure tends to not. This is also why cold fronts tend to be on the front of approaching high pressure systems, and warm fronts on the front of approaching low pressure areas.

Air pressure is also different at varying elevations. This is why it is important to focus on the elevation of where you are located in relation to your current air pressure. Air has less pressure pressing on it the higher you get in elevation.

Chapter 3 : Weather Application

Applying what you have learned and observed in weather is the final step to creating a forecast or to finish your data for record-keeping. The data collection part of meteorology is very simple, however, it does serve as the backbone for everything you do concerning your studies. Applying that data to create a forecast will take a little bit more work to do and is a bit more rewarding than seeing just a data sheet.

To create a forecast or educated weather opinion, you will need to first translate your data into a cleaner, easier to understand format. Forecasters will do this by making graphs and graphics to display their data in a pretty and eye-catching way. There is no reason you can't do the same thing. Normally this is done in a program like Microsoft Power Point for use on a computer or television program. This book is not to teach you how to use power point, but I can attest to the power of it. It is an amazing tool that can help put your data into an eye-catching format that makes it looks professional. Tutorials exist all over the internet to learn to use this tool, however it is an expensive program as part of the Office Suite. You can explore for other way to display your information. There are several free art programs out on the internet that will allow you to put your data into a "pretty" format for display to others.

Another valuable resource are your friends. By acquiring a focus group of friends, they can help critique your work in a way that hurts less than having a professional attempt to tear it apart. Bringing in friends in this case will help you fix things and help cater your work to a bigger audience that will be looking to see the same things your friends are. Never underestimate the advice of a good friend when it comes to your work or passion.

The best advice I can give when it comes to creating an image and name for yourself is to stay within your comfort zone when creating your impression. Too many forecasters attempt to gimmick their work and become a personality they are not and often get caught out for not being authentic. People are looking for those who they can trust with their weather. Trust is a huge asset that many forecasters are slowly losing due to botched forecasts and bad interpersonal appeal. Learning to accept when you are wrong and admitting so to those that look for your work is a big step in creating a rapport with them. They are going to know you are wrong, however, telling them so will let them know you take great pride in your work and will correct the mistakes that may have occurred.

You might also want to refrain from having arguments with your fellow meteorologists and weather enthusiasts. The reason for this is obvious. You do not want to appear to be a combative person that is not open to other's opinions. Weather is an evolving science that still has a lot to be discovered concerning it. Take others opinions into account even if they seem to upset you. After all, they have read your opinion or forecast and now have a response. If the words are bad and do not warrant a response, it is best to leave it alone until the person comes up with a better formulated response. Work with people to help them understand your material, do not automatically declare that you are totally right and won't budge.

This section really isn't as much to help your career as it is to help focus your studies and aspirations of weather. Some people are very passionate about this subject and can become easily offended when it comes to someone corrupting their understanding of it. So, it is important to find that happy medium because people like that will help you learn higher degrees of knowledge when it comes to thermodynamics and meteorology.

Creating your image and presence in the community is very simple as long as you are willing to take everyone's concepts into account. At the same time, promote your ideas as well, and back them up with educated data and talk. This way, when someone has a question or has a disagreement with you, you can back up your conversation with some viable information rather than declaring that you automatically

know what you are saying with no logical
backup.

Be aware that the prior sections of this
book have served has nothing more than a basic
understanding of the world of weather, and that
there are a lot more advanced topics out there
in this subject. Hurricanes, tornadoes, and
even floods have their own sets of dynamics,
and I have written books about these more
advanced subjects. This is a reference guide
for those of you who wish to start your studies
and enter into the world of weather… or for
long time professionals looking for a reference
book to use while in the field. For both of you
I have compiled this book to give you an easy
resource when those data connections don't work
so well.

Field Tips for your Journey

You may be very anxious to get out into the field and do some physical data recording and weather forecasting. However, you might want to adhere to a few tips that will allow you to have fun and remain safe while observing the weather. Nature is ferocious and unpredictable, and can often turn against you if you fail to heed warning signs.

When recording data and observing thunderstorms, it is important to note that if you can hear thunder then you are close enough to it to be struck by lightning. Lightning is one of nature's #1 killers and often is regarded lightly during observation sessions. Lightning can strike from a cloud over 12 miles away, so be aware that you could be struck. If you find yourself with the warning signs of hair rising on the back of your next or a tingling sensation on softer tissues of your body, the best thing to do is to curl up and put your knees to your chest and place your head into your arms and hold them against your legs. This will allow the current to pass as safely through your body as it can. By giving the current less area to run through, and bypassing your heart, the danger to you may be some burns. Seek medical attention immediately after experiencing a lightning strike. Also, do not stand underneath trees or higher objects during thunderstorms.

Hail is also a danger during thunderstorms. Larger hail can dent cars, break windows, and cause large amounts of damage. It can also cause concussions and bruises if caught out in the storm. If you have to be outside when large hail is falling, try to wear the proper equipment, or buy a hardhat for use when dealing with these types of events. A hardhat can also help protect your head during stronger wind events.

When experiencing a severe thunderstorm, stay away from windows just in case a strong wind gust throws an object through it. Shattered glass can severely cut your skin and get into your eyes. Also be aware that lightning can sometimes find its way through a window and strike the object close to it. By keeping yourself out of harm's way, you will prevent any accidents from occurring.

If you choose to storm chase, and are not educated by a skywarn class, please be advised that this is a very dangerous path to take. Even if you do not end up being injured, you may jeopardize the safety of others trying to effectively convey the correct information to emergency officials. Storm chasing is not just a hobby, it is a way for weather officials to have eyes on a potentially dangerous storm and to issue warnings properly to save lives.

Winter time can pose many hazards to you. Shoveling causes a lot of deaths each year because of strain placed on the heart of the elderly, or those who do not shovel correctly.

Never try to shovel more than you can easily pick up. Take frequent breaks, and make sure that if the snow is a heavier variety that you seek the help of others. Also be aware that if you shovel areas regularly during a storm, it prevents the rapid build up of snow and allows each shoveling session to be manageable, rather than one big scoop. Another danger during the winter is heavy snow and ice sticking to trees and homes and causing them to snap or become damaged. The best way to defend yourself against this is to stay away from buckling branches and power lines.

Ice and snow causes hazardous road conditions during the winter, do it is best to slow down and take extra time to get to your destination. Try to keep several car lengths of space between you and someone else while traveling the highway, and if possible use your caution lights to alert other motorists that you are moving slower than normal traffic. Also be aware that these hazards may be more dangerous at night, when they become much more difficult to detect. If you come upon a motorist who is driving dangerously for the conditions, back away from that driver the best you can to prevent you from becoming a part of any accident that driver causes.

As always, heed all watches and warnings issued by the National Weather Service. Try to avoid hype or situations presented by your local media, the best course of action is to wait for the official warning or advisory to be issued by the NWS.

Essential Weather Reference Guide

<u>Weather Tools/Devices</u>

Term	Definition
Anemometer	A tool used to measure the speed of winds at ground level. Some even show you wind direction.
Barometer	Device used to record air pressure at ground level. Units can be Inches/Mercury or Millibars.
Bulb (Wet)	A device used to record humidity of the air outside.
Sling Psychrometer	Measures relative humidity in the air. Uses two thermometers, swing one of them around and measures evaporation from a cloth.
Rain Gauge	Measures the amount of rain that has fallen

	since emptied.
Computer Models	These contain valuable information derived from data records around the world. Common models are GFS, ECMWF, NAM, and GEM.
Weather Balloon	These are released from reporting stations to collect atmospheric data that normally would not be accessible. They are a large buoyant balloon with a radiosonde device attached.
Radiosonde	This device contains a package of common weather recording devices that are collected by an onboard computer and relayed through radio signal back to a station.
Dropsonde	Much like a radiosonde, this is a package of weather recording tools, however, instead of being sent into the air they are dropped from a plane into developing storms.

Observation Buoy	These are buoys that are stations in various areas of the world's oceans. The relay back important ocean conditions to an observation station for processing. Until the use of orbiting satellites, this was the most effective way to spot large scale storms.
Satellites/IR	Orbiting the Earth, these high tech gadgets collect images of the weather within their view in several different spectrums. In dark conditions, their IR sensors capture images of dangerous weather in complete darkness.
Compass	A very low tech device, but can help pinpoint the direction a storm of event is coming from and also aid you in remaining away from dangerous weather.
Ruler/Yardstick	Measuring devices used for events which

	require a much large unit of measurement. Snowfall and some hail storms require the use of these devices in order to accurately gauge the severity of the situation.
High FPS Camera	Used to take a large amount of pictures of an area over a period of time. This technically allows the viewer to see events that may have gone by too fast to see. Often times these cameras are used to record lightning from thunderstorms.
Dopplar Radar	This device emits a signal into the air that bounces off any object that reflects its wavelength. Normally used for displaying areas of precipitation. With upgrade of Dual-Pol, it can now discern the precipitation type as well as intensity.

Ph Kit	Normally used to test the toxicity and balance of acidity in lakes and rivers, this tool is used to test acidity inside of rainwater contained in a rain gauge. A presence of high ph could mean you have been experiencing acid rain.
Mask	A flue mask that makes it easier to keep blowing sand and dirt out of your nose and mouth.
Safety Glasses	Keeps heavy rains, blowing sand and dirt out of your eyes.
Base Velocity Radar	Used to measure winds entering and exiting the radar site and how fast they are moving. Because winds of opposing directions show up as different colors, this is also used to detect storm rotation and tornadoes.

Forecaster Terms

Microcast : This is a tool that was created by forecasters to simulate the results of a computer model on a smaller scale for a local area. It uses images created by themselves, not actual computer models, collaged together to form an animation showing the possibility of an event or forecast.

Skew-T Chart: These charts are produced using data from weather balloons and compiled together to give a better understanding of the conditions in each layer of the atmosphere. The chart contains wind speed and direction as well as shear and temperatures in all levels of the atmosphere that the balloon has sampled. This can often help figure out what precipitation types may fall, as well as if there is any spin for supercell storms to form. Valuable in creating forecasts for certain time periods.

300mb: These are conditions located about 30,000 feet in elevation.

500mb: Conditions located at 18,000 feet into the atmosphere. This is an important layer because it sits near the divergence area in the atmosphere and contains accuracy in vorticity of storm systems.

700mb: Located at 10,000 feet into the atmosphere. Used to locate steering winds.

850mb: This layer represents the top of the planetary boundary layer, sitting at 5000 feet. This layer influences the temperatures in the lower layers much more than any other. So thi9s layer is typically used to locate areas of dense and non-dense air and can often help pinpoint the constant fight between precipitation types.

1000mb: This layer is located at sea surface level.

Jet Stream: This is a river of air created into the atmosphere by the rising of thermal gradients throughout the world and are moved and warped by areas of high and low pressure. This layer typically sits between 200-300mb in the atmosphere (30k-50k) feet into the atmosphere. Some areas of this stream may be faster than others, but it tends to be a universal steering current for weather in many areas.

Trough: This tends to denote a large dip in the jet stream caused by a low pressure system pulling the winds into a more south to north orientation. This typically traps a high pressure area in its wake, allowing this cold air to push the main storm system along.

Ridge: A ridge is a large bulge in the jet stream typically caused by a high pressure system. This typically switches the orientation of the wind in front of it into a more north to south orientation.

Cut-Off Low: Sometimes a low pressure system will form in an area not dictated by the constant flow of the jet stream. Hence the steering currents with this system are completely missing, and they tend to wobble about under direction of their own air flow. This typically means that they do not move much until a stronger flow picks it up.

Upper-Level Low: This is a low trapped in the upper levels of the atmosphere, typically from 500mb to 700mb, that can produce some volatile weather. Because it is trapped in these layers, they typically don't affect much change upon surface observations but will still cause weather.

Squall Line: This is a line of storms that will typically form about 70-120 miles ahead of the main cold front. These storms are often spawned off the outflow of old thunderstorms and contain gusty winds due to creating their own outflow boundaries.

Outflow Boundary: This is an area of winds created by dying or long dead storms. New thunderstorms like to form along the edges of these boundaries because they provide lower pressure and plenty of lift. Not dangerous on their own, it is not until they start producing the additional storms that they become violent.

Derecho: These feature are typically referred to as "land hurricanes" because the squall lines associate with them can produce very strong sustained winds, and travel for over 150 miles. Some of these derecho features can develop a mesocyclonic feature at their head. A derecho has a very specific set of guidelines which include intensity and duration as well as distance traveled. Under current understanding a line of storms must travel 175 miles while producing winds of 75+ MPH to be considered a derecho. Sometimes leeway is granted in classifying this type of system, even though it is not warranted.

Lake-Effect: This typically occurs when the Great Lakes are warmer than the air moving over them. They release moisture into the air which is picked up by the resulting colder air and deposited on the opposite side. The wind must be blowing over the lake in order for this to occur, and the area affected will depend on which direction the wind is blowing from.

Ocean-Effect: This occurs much the same as lake effect. However, the air comes off the ocean and enhances precipitation over the area, normally from a bay of some sort. This also requires the absence of a stabilizing marine layer.

Gust Front: Associated with powerful outflow winds from thunderstorms, this is a line of winds that extend over a large area. These winds can kick up dirt and dust and become Gustnadoes, which are simple winds that have debris within them. These gust fronts don't usually last very long, up to about 30 minutes at a time.

Surge (storm): Used to identify a pocket of water that has been pushed ahead of a storm due to strong winds. The surge is a rise of water in addition to normal tides and wave action. This aspect of a storm is typically the most dangerous.

Risk/Classification Charts

Enhanced Fujita Scale (Tornadoes)

Rank (EF)	Winds(3-second gust)
0	65-85 Mph
1	86-110 Mph
2	111-135 Mph
3	136-165 Mph
4	166-200 Mph
5	201+ Mph

Winds are measured both by physical indicators and Doppler radar stations.

Saffir-Simpson Scale (Hurricanes)

Rank	Winds(1-min Sustained)

Depression	<38 Mph
Storm	38-73 Mph
Category 1	74-95 mph (64-82 kts)
Category 2	96-110 mph(83-95 kts)
Category 3	111-130 mph(96-113 kts)
Category 4	131-155 mph(114-135 kts
Category 5	>155 mph (>135 kts)

Winds are measured over a 60 second time frame. Values above are maximum sustained values found inside circulation.

Nor'Easter and Blizzard Types

Miller-A: This classification essentially means that the storm has formed of a single low pressure system with very little influence from any other dynamics. Miller-A storms don't typically "phase', which means to transfer energy from one low pressure area to another.

Miller-B: This type of storm uses 2 or more areas of low pressure to form into a larger entity. Typical results from multiple areas of low pressure can "phase" into a new low off of coastal areas, intensifying rapidly to form a larger storm. These storms typically have a wide range of dynamics at play.

HECS (Historic East Coast Storm): This classification can be used with either a Miller A or B type storm and has more to do with impact potential than anything else. Typically this denotation is used when a storm would impact an area so dangerously that it would be labeled historic.

Nor'Easter: This is a term used for a storm that takes a track that brings a northeast wind into the New England area. This wind direction is typically cold and moist, bringing moisture in off of Atlantic Ocean around Cape Cod Massachusetts. This storm denotation does not necessarily mean a snowstorm, however. It just denotes the overall wind direction from the storm.

Blizzard: In order for a storm to be classified as a blizzard it much produce sustained winds over a 3-6 hour period of at least 35 mph. It also must contain heavy falling or blowing snow. Also visibility must remain at a ¼ mile or less for 3-6 hours. This means that you don't even have to have snow falling for a blizzard to occur. However, weather forecasters typically call those that have no falling snow "Ground Blizzards".

Winter Storm: This is a typical snow event that produces in excess of 6 inches of snow in a short amount of time. 6 inches of snow is enough to disrupt travel and operations in larger cities, so it becomes a dangerous event.

Often times forecasters will not even consider a snow event a Winter Storm unless the snowfall total reaches at least 10 inches in a 12-18 hour period.

Thunderstorm Classifications

Thunderstorm: A cumulonimbus cloud formation typically with an anvil top that produces heavy rain and lightning.

Strong Storm: This is a stronger version of a thunderstorm that can typically produce hail less than 1 inch in diameter and winds less than 58 mph.

Severe Storm: This is a thunderstorm capable of producing hail in excess of 1 inch in diameter, winds greater than 58 mph. These storms typically have frequent cloud-to-ground lightning and very heavy rain.

Tornadic Storm: These are storms that have an associated funnel cloud that has been spotted by trained weather spotters. These storms tend to trigger tornado warnings until their rotation subsides.

Supercell: These types of storms are single cloud storms that have rotation around their entire perimeter. Often times these storms peak the interest of storm chasers because they tend to produce tornadoes thanks to strong updrafts and rotation already present within the storm.

These types of storms are very common in the plains states in the U.S. , however, they can occur almost anywhere in the world. These formations can produce heavy rain, or almost no rain at all. Normally these storms tend to form along the boundaries of dry air, and are single cell. This means that they rarely have an attached line of storms associated with it.

Squall Line: This is a line of thunderstorm activity that usually forms ahead of the main cold front. These storms like to form along the outflow boundaries of storms located behind them, and are gusty type thunderstorms that can contain heavy winds. These quick moving storms are often short-lived and fizzle just as quickly as they form, as the atmosphere stabilizes around them with the loss of daytime heating.

Advisory Guide

Hazardous Weather Advisory: These statements are issued when conditions could produce adverse effects that can slow down or cause mild danger to those in the advisory area.

Wind Advisory: Issued when winds are between 25 to 39 miles per hour sustained, or gusts up to 57 mph. This is site specific and does not apply to areas that typically see winds of this speed as a common occurrence.

High Wind Warning: These warnings are issued when sustained winds over a land area exceed 39 mph sustained or over 57 mph with gusts. However, these are not associated with tropical systems or brief events like thunderstorms.

Hurricane Force Wind Warning: This is issued when winds are expected to continuously gust over hurricane force (74 mph) over the warning area. This is not the same as a Hurricane Warning, and aren't involved with tropical advisories.

Flood Watch: This watch is issued when there poses a potential of flooding for a specific area. This does not mean areas are flooding, this means that the conditions exist for flooding to occur at some point.

Flood Warning: This warning means that flooding is being observed in areas of the affected zone and that you should be mindful of this occurring. This normally happens when a few days of rain empties into a river and causes the water level to gradually rise.

Flash Flood Watch: This means that conditions may exist within the next few hours of heavy rain to cause rapid water rise in the area. This does not mean it is occurring, it just means there is a possibility for it to occur as a result of an event.

Flash Flood Warning: This is issued when a storm or heavy rain event prompts a rapid rise of water in an area. Poor drainage and low lying areas may enhance this possibility, but it also means that there is flash flooding already occurring somewhere in the affected area.

Areal Flood Watch: This is about the same as a Flood Watch, however, the flood possibility area is much larger than a flood warning area. Areal Flood Watches can include areas far outside the zone of a flood watch, and may experience effects of the flood zones as a result of water rise farther away than anticipated. Flood warnings will be issued as normal for these areas if conditions deteriorate to flood stage.

Severe Thunderstorm Watch: This watch means that conditions are ripe for strong thunderstorm development that could possibly turn severe. Conditions must be supportive of severe development for this type of watch to be issued.

Severe Thunderstorm Warning: This means that a severe thunderstorm is in progress in an area contained in the warning area. These warnings will only be issued once a thunderstorm reaches a certain strength and will be updated continuously to monitor the potential severe storm.

Tornado Watch: This is issued for an area that contains conditions that are ripe for tornadic storm development. Storms in the area may have conditions to cause rotation within the storms, so this watch is issued to alert people of the possibility.

Tornado Warning: This means the area has a tornado on the ground or circulation possible of producing a tornado has been spotted within the area and you are to take cover immediately. This does not mean a tornado is necessarily in progress, this means that a storm capable of dropping a tornado at any moment is within the area of the warning. Normally a siren will sound in your community, letting you know to seek shelter immediately.

Red Flag Warning: This means that conditions outside are very dry, allowing vegetation and other objects to be devoid of moisture, presenting a greatly increased fire danger. Heed these warnings and do not do open burns or discard extremely hot or smoldering items in these areas. This also can denote areas with increased winds around fires already burning, prompting dangerous warning ahead of them as they spread.

Dense Fog Advisory: These are issued when fog lowers visibility to below half a mile in the advisory area. This prevents you from seeing the normal distance while driving and can pose a danger on highways and areas close to water. Lakes and rivers tend to enhance the effects of fog with extra moisture, so these areas may be much more dense than others.

Winter Weather Advisory: These are produced when winter time conditions exist in an area, but fall below winter storm criteria. These are also issued when noticeable icing effects are to affect an area. Areas in these advisories are to watch for dangers caused by winter time weather but should not expect a large snowstorm.

Winter Storm Watch: This watch is prompted when an area has the potential to see 6 inches of snow or more, or significant icing within a storm. These watches are prompted 12-48 hours before a storm arrival if confidence exists that an area will see these conditions. These watches usually precede the storm and become upgraded within 24 hours of its arrival.

Winter Storm Warning: This warning is issued when the possibility of 6 inches or more of snow, or significant icing of greater than ¼ inch exists within the next 24 hours. Sometimes these warnings are held back until 12 hours before an event due to lower confidence.

Blizzard Watch: This watch is issued when confidence of a snow event producing heavy snow, sustained winds of 35 mph or more, blowing or drifting snow, and visibilities below ¼ mile for 3-6 hours are a possibility. Just like a winter storm watch, this watch is typically issued 12-48 hours before the event.

Blizzard Warning: This warning is issued when conditions of heavy/blowing snow, winds of 35+ mph, and visibility ¼ or less are expected within 12-24 hours. When issued, these means confidence is high that an event like this will occur within the warning period.

Tropical Storm Watch: These watches are issued when winds of tropical storm force (39-73 mph) have a potential of reaching the area within 24-48 hours. Preparations to protect property should be underway once this watch is issued.

Tropical Storm Warning: This warning is issued when winds of tropical storm force (39-73 mph) are expected to affect the area within the next 24 hours. Preparations to protect property should be complete once this warning is issued.

Hurricane Watch: This watch is posted for areas that have a possibility of seeing hurricane force winds (74+ mph) affecting their area within the next 24-48 hours. Preparations to protect life and property should be underway once this watch is issued.

Hurricane Warning: This warning is issued when the confidence of seeing hurricane force winds (74+ mph) within the next 12-24 hours are very high. Any preparations to protect life and property should be complete at this point and you should be seeking shelter.

Heavy Surf Advisory: This is issued when wave heights are much higher than normal and cause extra beach erosion and rip current dangers. Heed these advisories if heading to an ocean adjacent beach.

Coastal Flood Warning: This is issued when tide heights are expected to be higher than normal due to a storm or offshore event. The tide cycle can add extra height onto these warnings as well. Areas close to ocean facing beaches and low lying coastal areas should heed these warnings very carefully.

Heat Advisory: These are issued when heat index values in areas that typically don't see hot temperatures exceed 105 degrees F. These areas must be above 105 but less than 115 for 3 or more hours during an advisory day. Also, a heat advisory can be issued if an area sees nighttime low temperatures of 80+ for 2 or more consecutive days. Check on elderly neighbors and those with disabilities to ensure they do not suffer heat stroke or exhaustion.

Excessive Heat Watch: This watch occurs when conditions are expected to produce heat index values over 105F for 2 or more consecutive days, or values of 115+F at any point in time over the affected areas. These watches can be issued 12-24 hours ahead of time. If you are in this watch, prepare to have a way to cool off and bring plenty of water to where you go.

Excessive Heat Warning: This warning is issued when the heat index value for an area is greater than 105F for 2 consecutive days, or exceeds 115F for any period of time. These criteria can differ greatly from region to region and can be higher where these values are more common. Check on the elderly and those with disabilities.

Frost Advisory: This advisory is issued when temperatures overnight plummet to between 33-38F degrees, which allows condensation to crystalize on standing surfaces. Frost can damage tender plants left outside.

Freeze Warning: This warning is issued when the overnight temperature goes to 32F or below. This allows standing water to freeze, as well as severely damage any plants left outside uncovered.

Wind Chill Advisory: Values that prompt this advisory differ over areas, however, the advisory prompts you to wear warm clothing and layers to prevent frostbite.

Wind Chill Warning: This warning means dangerous wind chills as occurring. Values that prompt this warning are different from area to area, however, exposure of longer than 30 minutes to these conditions can cause frostbite and hypothermia.

Hard Freeze Warning: Usually when temperatures of less than 28F are expected in an area during the growing season are warmer seasons, a hard freeze advisory will be issued. Hard freeze can severely damage or kill off plants without frost.

/--\

Many other watches and warning exist, but are specialized products of the local officers of the National Weather Service. This means that the local area bases the watches and warnings on the local climate and weather patterns. Pay attention to any new weather watch products from your local NWS office, and learn what they mean.

Do not take any of these advisories, watches, or warnings lightly. They have been created by the National Weather Service in order to better help you (the public) understand when a potentially dangerous situation may be present or occurring. Taking action immediately upon issuance of these products may be the best course of action unless they have a long duration issuance.

\--/

Meteorology Reference Materials

Commonly Used Weather Calculations

Temperature

Celsius to Fahrenheit: F = 9/5 x(C)+32

Kelvin to Fahrenheit: F = 9/5(K-273)+32

Fahrenheit to Celsius: C = 5/9(F-32)

Celsius to Kelvin: K = C+273

Fahrenheit to Kelvin: K = 5/9(F-32)+273

Wind Chill: WC = 35.74 + 0.6215F - 35.75mph (**0.16) + 0.425FMph(**0.16)

Wind Speed

Kilometer to Mile: M = Km/1.61

Mile to Kilometer: Km = M*1.61

Acceleration: Acc = Distance/Time^2

Knots to Mph: MPH = Kts*1.15

Mph to Knots: Kts = MPH/1.15

Air Pressure

Inches(Hg) to Millibars(mb): mb = Hg*33.8639

Millibars(mb) to Inches(Hg): Hg = mb*0.02953

Important Weather Acronyms

NWS: Abbreviation for the National Weather service.

NHC: The National Hurricane Center. This locale handles tropical weather advisories and updates on tropical weather.

SPC: Storm Prediction Center. This division takes care of severe weather issuance and products based on severe weather probabilities.

NOAA: National Oceanic and Atmospheric Administration. Part of the U.S Department of Commerce, this agency is responsible for all weather related products and serves as a parent to the National Weather Service.

HP: High precipitation. A denotation of storms in general, this designates that the storm is producing large amounts of rain.

LP: Low precipitation. This designates that a storm is producing little to no precipitation.

PDS: Particularly Dangerous Situation. This is issued when an event or set of events prompts a quick and decisive response in warning the general public about the increased danger of that event. An example of a PDS would be a tornado outbreak.

WW: This designates a Weather Watch. Often times the National Weather Service will use this designation to quickly issue watches to particular areas.

MD: Short for Mesoscale Discussion. These are issued when particular areas will be experiencing a special or enhanced area of weather from the rest of the forecasted area. An example of this would a MD showing an area where severe storms are more likely to form within the watch area.

CG: This designates cloud to ground lightning strikes.

CC: Designates cloud to cloud lightning within a storm.

RFD: This is Rear Flank Downdraft, which is thought to be essential in the production of supercell tornadoes. This is an area of descending air at the rear of the thunderstorm that helps to spin the column of air that potentially causes a tornado.

FFD: Known as Forward Flank Downdraft, which is an area of cool and sometimes moist air flowing out of the front of a large thunderstorm.

540: This is typically referred to during the winter time as the line of freezing air in the 850mb level of the atmosphere. Normally this becomes what we know as the rain/snow line for areas across the country during winter storms. 540 stands for the height of the air within that layer. The lower the number, the colder the layer of air is in the 850mb zone.

LI: This stands for Lift index, which is a number that rates the buoyancy of the air in forming thunderstorms. The higher the number, the more likely the resulting air will form a thunderstorm if triggered.

GFS: Also known as the American Model, this weather processing forecast model is called Global Forecast System. This is one of many computer models used in the formulation of forecasts for many meteorologists.

ECMWF: This stands for European Centre for Medium-Range Weather Forecasts. Also known as the EURO, this forecast model is used along side the GFS system to help narrow down forecast errors, and to help build more accurate forecasts.

NAM: This is the North American Mesoscale model. This is usually the short range version of the GFS model, up to 84 hours out from a forecast period.

GEM: This is the Global Environmental Multiscale model, which Canada runs along side with the GFS to produce more accurate forecasts. Typically it is included into the

GFS model ensemble members to output at a better resolution.

GEFS: This stands for Global Ensemble Forecast System, and uses 22 member models to produce various outputs for a forecast. The outcome is averaged against each member and then put into the operation run of this model.

NAEFS: This stands for the North American Ensemble Forecast System. Using the GEFS, GFS, and GEM, this system combines all of these outputs to provide multiple member solutions to a forecast.

Z: This letter serves as a designation of "hour" by the weather world. If someone is talking about 12z, they are talking about wither a noontime run of a model, or the 12 hour panel of the specific model being represented.

HRRR: This stands for High Resolution Rapid Refresh model. This model takes and forecasts conditions on a smaller grid than other models, allowing it to pinpoint areas of disturbed weather. Also known as RAP or RR, this model goes out to 18 hours from its operational run.

MOS: This stands for Modeling Output Statistics. Used for model errors.

Common Weather Symbols

SYMBOL	DESIGNATION
H	HIGH PRESSURE
L	LOW PRESSURE
	COLD FRONT

	WARM FRONT
	OCCLUDED FRONT
	STATIONARY FRONT
	TROPICAL STORM

	HURRICANE
	SUNNY
	SUN/CLOUDS
	CLOUDY
	RAIN

	SNOW
	WINDY
	THUNDERSTORM

**SYMBOLS ABOVE MAY DIFFER FROM ICONS
THAT YOUR LOCAL FORECAST OFFICE USES**

Hurricane Preparation Guide

Every year hurricanes put millions of people at risk along the east and west coasts of the United States. By following this simple guide you can cut down the risks to your home, and be prepared in case of emergencies.

Protecting Your Home

---

1. Use plywood to cover up any glass on the exterior of your home. Debris and wind can break this glass and send it hurtling through the air.

2. Secure any freestanding furniture or objects based around the exterior of your home. If you can bring it inside your home, then do so. Use strong rope to secure the objects and try to keep them as low profile as possible, keeping large surfaces away from the wind direction.

3. Ensure your storm drains and piping around your home is free of clutter and debris that may clog them during a heavy rain event. If you see a cluttered drain on your roadway, it may be a good thing to attempt to clear it.

---

4. Basements may flood, so ensure that your basement is properly sealed from the outside elements, to protect valuables inside. If you cannot seal the basement in adequate time, then move whatever you wish to save to higher ground.

5. Loose and overhanging branches can cause a lot of damage to your home in hurricanes. Try to recognize these and trim them up or remove them before an event. If branches overhang your power lines, try to contact your utility company about removing these branches before they pose a power risk.

6. No matter how well you protect your home, flying debris from other homes and businesses are bound to damage your home during an event. It is best to make sure your insurance is up to date and covers your home in case of this type of event. Also purchase flood insurance to insure your home is protected in case of high waters.

7. Make sure your generator has plenty of gas if it requires it. If you are going to use your generator to power aspects of your home, you are going to need enough gasoline to power those things for 3-7 days. Running the generator intermittently is the best way to conserve gasoline. Try running the

generator for an hour at a time, then
giving it a rest for an hour.

Hurricane Emergency Kit

The best way to get through a hurricane
is to have an emergency kit prepared in case
you either get stuck at home or are forced to
evacuate. The contents of this kit will depends
on whether you are stuck in your home or
evacuating.

---

1. Enough water per person (1 gallon per
   person/day) for 3 to 7 days inside the
   home.

2. A supply of non-perishable food depending
   on family size.

3. Children's necessities (diapers, formula,
   wipes) if you have a baby.

4. A Manual can opener. Remember,
   electricity may be out for days!

5. A first aid kit that contains bandages,
   antiseptic, and other essential supplies.
   This can be purchased at a store
   relatively cheap and will contain first
   aid essentials.

---

6. Prescription medications. Ensure that all prescription medicines are stored in their plastic containers to keep moisture out.

7. Toiletries. This means soap, deodorant, washcloths, toilet paper, and other things.

8. Cell phone and chargers for those phones that run on batteries. If the electricity is out you will not be able to charge your phone. If you are stuck in your home, you may need to use the phone to call for assistance after the hurricane.

9. Battery powered radio and flashlight. Having a weather radio helps you keep up to date with the conditions outside and the possibility of emergency assistance. Battery powered flashlights are recommended instead of candles. Often lighting candles can start fires in the home, and can also cause fire when they are blown or knocked over. Always use a flashlight over a candle.

10. A large supply of batteries for all of the things that require batteries to use. Make sure you have various sizes of batteries in case the things you need to power require different types.

11.   Make sure to have some cash on hand on your persons in case you need to leave the home after the storm. The ATMs will not be working if the power is out.

12.   Blankets, sleeping backs, some books and possibly games. This is important because you will need to sleep away from the walls of your home, and the games and books will provide something for bored people to do while riding out the storm.

If You Have been ordered to Evacuate

---

1. Bring non-perishable food for your family. Shelters may have water available, but they often do not have food.

2. Bring prescription medications with you in labeled bottles. Ensure you have at least a 7 day supply on hand.

3. Bring sleeping bags, blankets, books and games. Shelters will have an area for you to set up your sleeping arrangements, but you will need your own materials.

---

4. Know your evacuation route. Often times these will be marked by blue circular signs that read "Evacuation Route". Practice driving down these areas if you can so that you know the way to the nearest shelter.

5. Bring animals to the nearest animal housing or shelter for boarding. Do not leave your pet behind. Also bring a supply of pet food with you for 3-7 days to give to the shelter for your pet, as they most likely will not have a large supply of food on hand.

6. Be sure to turn your gas off at your home to prevent gas spillage if damage occurs while you are away.

7. If possible, turn power off by flipping your breaker switches before leaving the home, just to ensure that fire will not start from within the home via electricity surges.

8. Make sure to have a change of clothes or two for each member of your family. You do not want to be sweating around in your clothes too much.

9. Make sure your car is full of gasoline so that if evacuation takes a long time to process, you will not run out of gas.

10.   Most of all, do not panic. Panic only causes chaos and confusion. Your officials will let you know well ahead of time if you need to evacuate. Do not bring superfluous items with you as well. You might be able to charge your cell phone at the shelter, but do not expect to be able to plug in your gaming console.

Being safe and prepared is always the best way to get through an emergency situation. Apply both sides of the list here if evacuating, because sometimes shelters or areas that you need to evacuate to might not have these things readily available. If your officials tell you to evacuate, then you really should evacuate. Too many people have been killed or severely injured attempting to "ride out the storm" against their best intentions.

Also be sure to check your water supply for your family regularly, and dump them out and refill them at regular intervals. This prevents your family from drinking contaminated or filthy water. If you are at home, make sure you fill the bathtub up with water. This will allow you to use water in the tub for flushing the toilet if needed, and for hygienic purposes.

Overall, hurricanes are not storms to be messed with and cause tremendous amounts of

damage each year around the world. By being
prepared, you increase your odds of survival
into your favor. Remember, property and
objects can be replaced. You and your
family, however, cannot be replaced. Use
your brain and be safe.

Tornado Safety

Each year there are hundreds of tornadoes that occur in the United States, more than any other country in the world. Even though most of these tornadoes do occur in a strip called "Tornado Alley", these destructive storms can affect almost anywhere. Being prepared for what to do during a tornado warning can mean the difference between life and death.

---

1. If you area is under a tornado warning, you will need to react very fast to it and move you and your family to a basement shelter area. If you do not have a basement or shelter area, find a central room in your home like a bathroom or strong closet, and place a mattress or blanket over you and get as close to the ground as possible.

2. Stay Away from windows and other weak structures that can break or shatter and become airborne. Once the wind picks up this debris, it can become very dangerous in a hurry.

3. Winds within a tornado are very fast, and localized, meaning that sometimes you won't even hear the tornado coming

before it hits. The best thing to do is to assume that the tornado is going to hit your area once the warning is issued and protect yourself and family.

4. It is very often not recommended to enter your vehicle and attempt to outrun an approaching tornado. Roads may be damaged or covered with debris, making escape via vehicle next to impossible.

5. If you are caught outside during a tornado, find a low point in the terrain. This can be a ditch on the side of a roadway, or divot in the landscape. Keep your body close to the ground as you can and cover your head with your arms.

6. Due to the extremely unpredictable nature and quickness of tornado formation, you may not have very much time between the warning issuance and the tornado. Ensure you respond to the warning quickly, and do not waste any time foolishly protecting property.

7. If you can safely avoid the path of the tornado, please do so. Keep roadways close to the impact area free of vehicles and people so that

emergency crews from other towns can come to the aid of the affected areas.

8. It may take a day or two for rescue crews to locate where you are in the rubble, so be sure to continually call out to others to let them know where you are. If you have a working cell phone, call 911 and alert rescuers to exactly where you are located inside your home.

9. If you were not directly affected by the tornado, try to help crews outside your home to locate trapped people and dangerous areas. Any assistance you can give for them would be appreciated by the rescue crews.

10. Don't attempt to be superhuman and watch the tornado as it nears your home. These critical moments you spend watching the storm move towards you are seconds lost saving your life.

Given these bits of advice, tornadoes still sneak up on communities every year and causes catastrophic damage in those communities. No one can ever be fully prepared for this type of storm, however, you can ensure that by thinking quickly and acting just as quick you will be able to have a higher chance of survival.

If you can safely leave your home after a tornado hit, that would be the best choice of action. Dangers may still exist in your home after a strike, like collapsing floors, gas leaks, and electrical fires.

MELTWATER EQUIVALENT (INCHES)	NEW SNOWFALL (INCHES) Temperature (F)						
	34 to 28	27 to 20	19 to 15	14 to 10	9 to 0	-1 to -20	-21 to -40
trace	trace	0.1	0.2	0.3	0.4	0.5	1
0.01	0.1	0.2	0.2	0.3	0.4	0.5	1
0.02	0.2	0.3	0.4	0.6	0.8	1	2
0.03	0.3	0.5	0.6	0.9	1.2	1.5	3
0.04	0.4	0.6	0.8	1.2	1.6	2	4
0.05	0.5	0.8	1	1.5	2	2.5	5
0.06	0.6	0.9	1.2	1.8	2.4	3	6
0.07	0.7	1.1	1.4	2.1	2.8	3.5	7
0.08	0.8	1.2	1.6	2.4	3.2	4	8
0.09	0.9	1.4	1.8	2.7	3.6	4.5	9
0.1	1	1.5	2	3	4	5	10
0.11	1.1	1.7	2.2	3.3	4.4	5.5	11
0.12	1.2	1.8	2.4	3.6	4.8	6	12
0.13	1.3	2	2.6	3.9	5.2	6.5	13
0.14	1.4	2.1	2.8	4.2	5.6	7	14
0.15	1.5	2.3	3	4.5	6	7.5	15

New Wind Chill Chart

Wind Speed (mph)	Temperature (F)																	
0	40	35	30	25	20	15	10	5	0	-5	-10	-15	-20	-25	-30	-35	-40	-45
5	36	31	25	19	13	7	1	-5	-11	-16	-22	-28	-34	-40	-46	-52	-57	-63
10	34	27	21	15	9	3	-4	-10	-16	-22	-28	-35	-41	-47	-53	-59	-66	-72
15	32	25	19	13	6	0	-7	-13	-19	-26	-32	-39	-45	-51	-58	-64	-71	-77
20	30	24	17	11	4	-2	-9	-15	-22	-29	-35	-42	-48	-55	-61	-68	-74	-81
25	29	23	16	9	3	-4	-11	-17	-24	-31	-37	-44	-51	-58	-64	-71	-78	-84
30	28	22	15	8	1	-5	-12	-19	-26	-33	-39	-46	-53	-60	-67	-73	-80	-87
35	28	21	14	7	0	-7	-14	-21	-27	-34	-41	-48	-55	-62	-69	-76	-82	-89
40	27	20	13	6	-1	-8	-15	-22	-29	-36	-43	-50	-57	-64	-71	-78	-84	-91
45	26	19	12	5	-2	-9	-16	-23	-30	-37	-44	-51	-58	-65	-72	-79	-86	-93
50	26	19	12	4	-3	-10	-17	-24	-31	-38	-45	-52	-60	-67	-74	-81	-88	-95
55	25	18	11	4	-3	-11	-18	-25	-32	-39	-46	-54	-61	-68	-75	-82	-89	-97
60	25	17	10	3	-4	-11	-19	-26	-33	-40	-48	-55	-62	-69	-76	-84	-91	-98

HEAT INDEX CHART

High heat index values are a combination of temperature and humidity. For example, if the temperature is 95° and the relative humidity is 55%, the heat index temperature is 110°. Studies have shown that possible heat disorders which could affect people from these conditions include sunstroke, heat cramps and heat exhaustion. Heatstroke is possible with prolonged exposure and/or physical activity. People are urged to use common sense when pursuing outdoor activities.

To use this chart, simply read across from temperature scale on the left hand side to the intersecting relative humidity that is read across the top.

Relative Humidity (%)

Air Temperature	0	5	10	15	20	25	30	35	40	45	50	55	60	65	70	75	80	85	90	95	100
120	107	111	116	123	130	139	148														
115	103	107	111	115	120	127	135	143	151												
110	99	102	105	108	112	117	123	130	137	143	150										
105	95	97	100	102	105	109	113	118	123	129	135	142	149								
100	91	93	95	97	99	101	104	107	110	115	120	126	132	138	144						
95	87	88	90	91	93	94	96	98	101	104	107	110	114	119	124	130	136				
90	87	88	90	91	93	94	96	98	101	104	107	110	114	119	124	130	136				
85	76	79	80	81	82	83	84	85	86	87	88	89	90	91	93	95	97	99	102	102	108
80	73	74	75	76	77	77	78	79	79	80	81	81	82	83	85	86	86	87	88	89	91
75	69	69	70	71	72	72	73	73	74	74	75	75	76	76	77	77	78	78	79	79	80
70	64	64	65	65	66	66	67	67	68	68	69	69	70	70	70	70	71	71	71	71	72

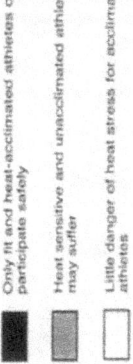

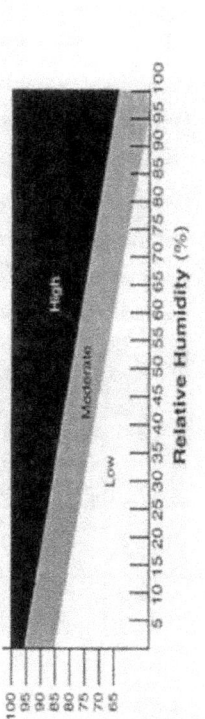

■ (black)	Only fit and heat-acclimated athletes can participate safely
■ (gray)	Heat sensitive and unacclimated athletes may suffer
□ (white)	Little danger of heat stress for acclimated athletes

Dewpoint Temperatures (°C)

Dry-Bulb Temperature (°C)	Difference Between Wet-Bulb and Dry-Bulb Temperatures (C°)														
	0	1	2	3	4	5	6	7	8	9	10	11	12	13	14	15
−20	−20	−33														
−18	−18	−28														
−16	−16	−24														
−14	−14	−21	−36													
−12	−12	−18	−28													
−10	−10	−14	−22													
−8	−8	−12	−18	−29												
−6	−6	−10	−14	−22												
−4	−4	−7	−12	−17	−29											
−2	−2	−5	−8	−13	−20											
0	0	−3	−6	−9	−15	−24										
2	2	−1	−3	−6	−11	−17										
4	4	1	−1	−4	−7	−11	−19									
6	6	4	1	−1	−4	−7	−13	−21								
8	8	6	3	1	−2	−5	−9	−14								
10	10	8	6	4	1	−2	−5	−9	−14	−28						
12	12	10	8	6	4	1	−2	−5	−9	−16						
14	14	12	11	9	6	4	1	−2	−5	−10	−17					
16	16	14	13	11	9	7	4	1	−1	−6	−10	−17				
18	18	16	15	13	11	9	7	4	2	−2	−5	−10	−19			
20	20	19	17	15	14	12	10	7	4	2	−2	−5	−10	−19		
22	22	21	19	17	16	14	12	10	8	5	3	−1	−5	−10	−19	
24	24	23	21	20	18	16	14	12	10	8	6	2	−1	−5	−10	−18
26	26	25	23	22	20	18	17	15	13	11	9	6	3	0	−4	−9
28	28	27	25	24	22	21	19	17	16	14	11	9	7	4	1	−3
30	30	29	27	26	24	23	21	19	18	16	14	12	10	8	5	1

Relative Humidity (%)

Dry-Bulb Temperature (°C)	Difference Between Wet-Bulb and Dry-Bulb Temperatures (C°)														
	0	1	2	3	4	5	6	7	8	9	10	11	12	13	14	15
−20	100	28														
−18	100	40														
−16	100	48														
−14	100	55	11													
−12	100	61	23													
−10	100	66	33													
−8	100	71	41	13												
−6	100	73	48	20												
−4	100	77	54	32	11											
−2	100	79	58	37	20	1										
0	100	81	63	45	28	11										
2	100	83	67	51	36	20	6									
4	100	85	70	56	42	27	14									
6	100	86	72	59	46	35	22	10								
8	100	87	74	62	51	39	28	17	6							
10	100	88	76	65	54	43	33	24	13	4						
12	100	88	78	67	57	48	38	28	19	10	2					
14	100	89	79	69	60	50	41	33	25	16	8	1				
16	100	90	80	71	62	54	45	37	29	21	14	7	1			
18	100	91	81	72	64	56	48	40	33	26	19	12	6			
20	100	91	82	74	66	58	51	44	36	30	23	17	11	5		
22	100	92	83	75	68	60	53	46	40	33	27	21	15	10	4	
24	100	92	84	76	69	62	55	49	42	36	30	25	20	14	9	4
26	100	92	85	77	70	64	57	51	45	39	34	28	23	18	13	9
28	100	93	86	78	71	65	59	53	47	42	36	31	26	21	17	12
30	100	93	86	79	72	66	61	55	49	44	39	34	29	25	20	16

[123]

Cloud Types

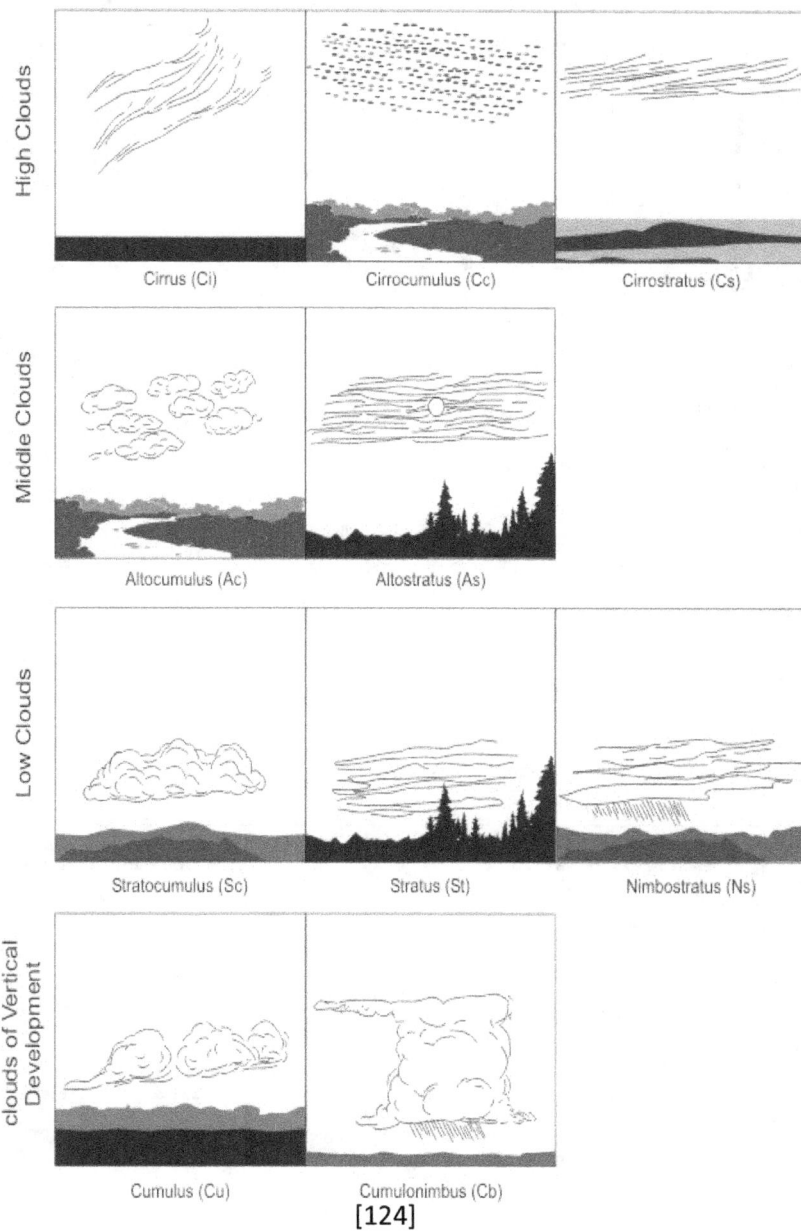

High Clouds

Cirrus (Ci)

Cirrocumulus (Cc)

Cirrostratus (Cs)

Middle Clouds

Altocumulus (Ac)

Altostratus (As)

Low Clouds

Stratocumulus (Sc)

Stratus (St)

Nimbostratus (Ns)

clouds of Vertical Development

Cumulus (Cu)

Cumulonimbus (Cb)

[124]

Weather Station Symbols

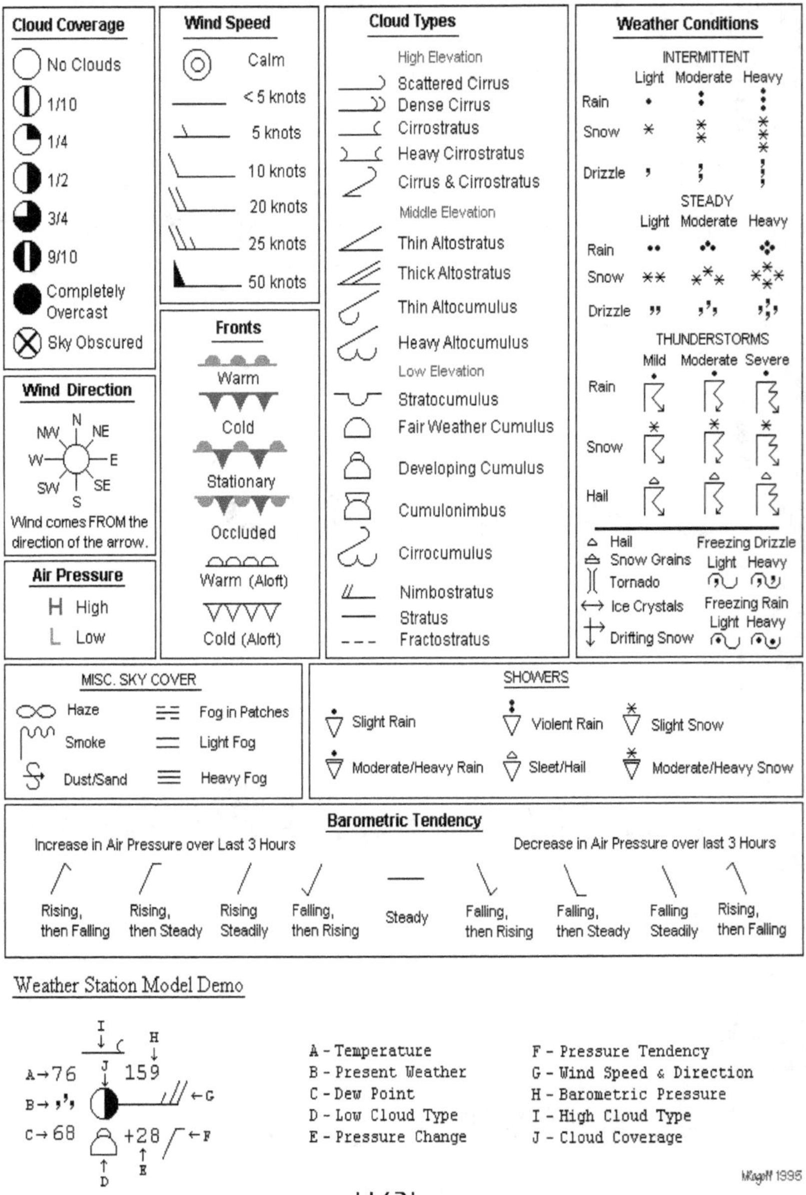

Cloud Coverage

- ◯ No Clouds
- ◑ 1/10
- ◕ 1/4
- ◑ 1/2
- ◕ 3/4
- ◖ 9/10
- ● Completely Overcast
- ⊗ Sky Obscured

Wind Direction

NW N NE
W — E
SW S SE

Wind comes FROM the direction of the arrow.

Air Pressure

- H High
- L Low

Wind Speed

- ⊙ Calm
- — < 5 knots
- ⊣ 5 knots
- ⊥ 10 knots
- ⊥⊥ 20 knots
- ⊥⊥⊣ 25 knots
- ▙ 50 knots

Fronts

Warm
Cold
Stationary
Occluded
Warm (Aloft)
Cold (Aloft)

Cloud Types

High Elevation
- Scattered Cirrus
- Dense Cirrus
- Cirrostratus
- Heavy Cirrostratus
- Cirrus & Cirrostratus

Middle Elevation
- Thin Altostratus
- Thick Altostratus
- Thin Altocumulus
- Heavy Altocumulus

Low Elevation
- Stratocumulus
- Fair Weather Cumulus
- Developing Cumulus
- Cumulonimbus
- Cirrocumulus
- Nimbostratus
- Stratus
- Fractostratus

Weather Conditions

INTERMITTENT

	Light	Moderate	Heavy
Rain			
Snow			
Drizzle			

STEADY

	Light	Moderate	Heavy
Rain			
Snow			
Drizzle			

THUNDERSTORMS

	Mild	Moderate	Severe
Rain			
Snow			
Hail			

- △ Hail
- ⬠ Snow Grains
-)(Tornado
- ↔ Ice Crystals
- ↓ Drifting Snow

- Freezing Drizzle
- Freezing Rain — Light Heavy

MISC. SKY COVER

- ∞ Haze
- ⌇ Smoke
- Ƨ Dust/Sand
- ⚌ Fog in Patches
- ⚊ Light Fog
- ☰ Heavy Fog

SHOWERS

- ▽ Slight Rain
- ▽ Violent Rain
- ▽ Slight Snow
- ▽ Moderate/Heavy Rain
- ▽ Sleet/Hail
- ▽ Moderate/Heavy Snow

Barometric Tendency

Increase in Air Pressure over Last 3 Hours

Decrease in Air Pressure over last 3 Hours

Rising, then Falling	Rising, then Steady	Rising Steadily	Falling, then Rising	Steady	Falling, then Rising	Falling, then Steady	Falling Steadily	Rising, then Falling

Weather Station Model Demo

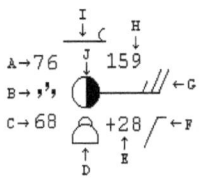

A → 76
B → ,',
c → 68

A – Temperature	F – Pressure Tendency
B – Present Weather	G – Wind Speed & Direction
C – Dew Point	H – Barometric Pressure
D – Low Cloud Type	I – High Cloud Type
E – Pressure Change	J – Cloud Coverage

Magoff 1995

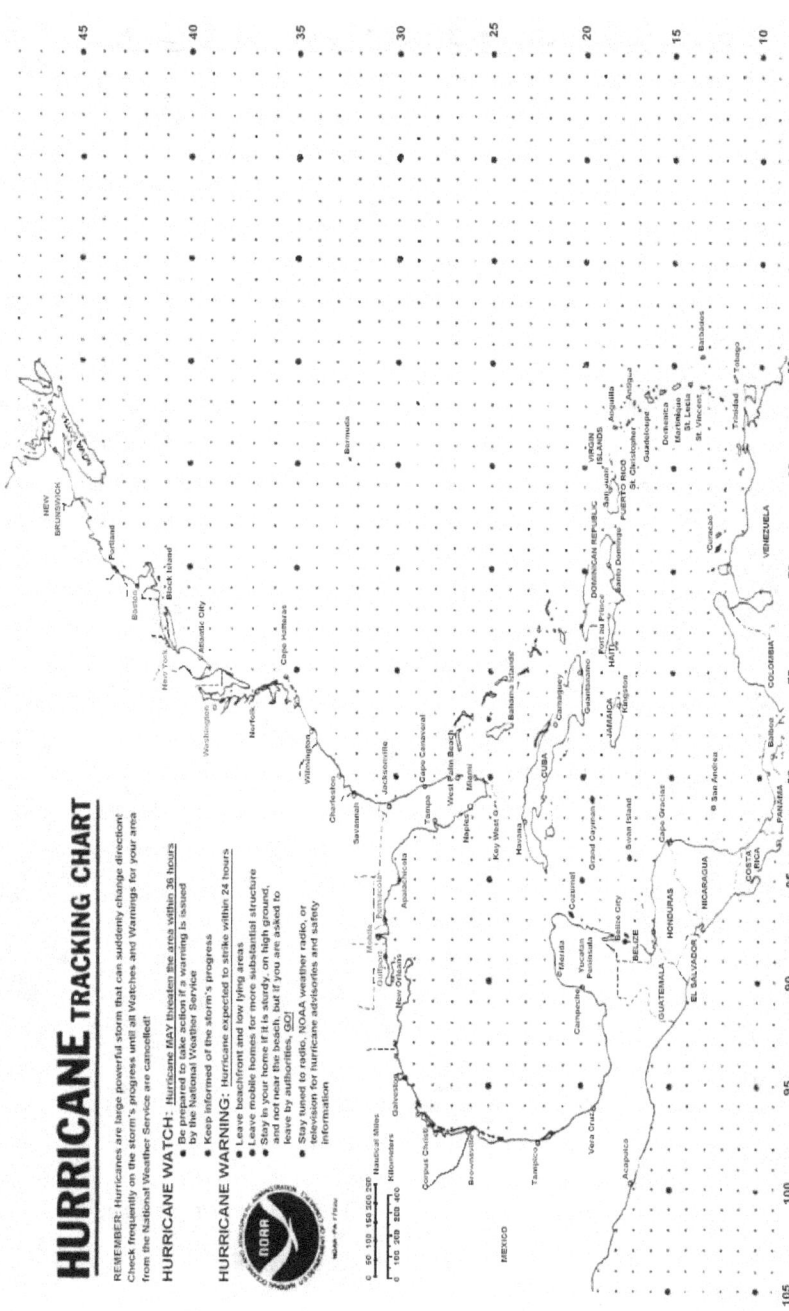

HURRICANE TRACKING CHART

REMEMBER: Hurricanes are large powerful storm that can suddenly change direction! Check frequently on the storm's progress until all Watches and Warnings for your area from the National Weather Service are cancelled!

HURRICANE WATCH: Hurricane MAY threaten the area within 36 hours

- Be prepared to take action if a warning is issued by the National Weather Service
- Keep informed of the storm's progress.

HURRICANE WARNING: Hurricane expected to strike within 24 hours

- Leave beachfront and low lying areas
- Leave mobile homes for more substantial structure
- Stay in your home if it is sturdy, on high ground, and not near the beach, but if you are asked to leave by authorities, GO!
- Stay tuned to radio, NOAA weather radio, or television for hurricane advisories and safety information

Conversions/Equations Listing

1° Latitude=

69.125 miles

Temp(F)=

Tf= (1.8*Tc)+32

Temp(C)=

Tc= (Tf-32)/1.8

Kelvin(Tk)=

Tk= 273.15 + Tc

Temp (Reamur) =

(25/36)(°F-32)

Temp (Rankine) =

°F + 459.67

Knots=

Knots= Wind Speed MPH * 0.868976241091

MPH=

MPH= Knots * 1.15077944802

Miles=

MI= Kilometers *

	0.6214
Kilometers=	KM= Miles * 1.61
Kilometers=	KM= Meters / 1000
Meters=	Meters= Kilometers * 1000
Meters=	M= Feet * 0.305
Meters Per Second=	M/S= Knots * 0.5148
Feet=	Ft= Meters*3.2808
Inches=	IN= CM / 2.54
Centimeters=	CM = IN * 2.54
Pascals(Pa)=	Pa= (Mb*100)

Kilopascal (Kp)=	Kp= InHg * 3.38638815789
Millibars(Mb)(Hectopascal) =	Mb= (In*33.86388158)
Inches of Mercury(InHg)=	InHg= (Mb/33.86388158)
Dew Point(F) Knowing Tc=	X= 1-(0.01*RH) K= Tc-(14.55+0.114*Tc)*X-((2.5+0.007*Tc)*X)^3-(15.9+0.117*Tc)*X^14 Tdf= (K*1.8)+32
Dew Point(F) Knowing Tf=	Tdf= ((((Tf-32)/1.8)-(14.55+0.114*((Tf-32)/1.8))*(1-(0.01*RH))-((2.5+0.007*((Tf-32)/1.8))*(1-(0.01*RH)))^3-(15.9+0.117*((Tf-32)/1.8))*(1-(0.01*RH))^14)*1.8)+32

[129]

Before Winter 2001/2002 Wind Chill(F)=	Wc= 0.0817*(3.71*SQRT(WIND SPEED MPH)+ 5.81-0.25*WIND SPEED MPH)*(Tf-91.4)+91.4
Starting Winter 2001/2002 Wind Chill °F = T = Air Temperature °F V = Wind Speed MPH	35.74 + 0.6215 * T - 35.75(V ^ 0.16) + 0.4275 * T (V ^ 0.16)
Heat Index(HI)=	HI= -42.379 + 2.04901523(Tf) + 10.14333127 (RH) - 0.22475541(Tf)(RH) - 6.83783x10^(-3)*(Tf^(2)) - 5.481717x10**(-2)*(RH^(2)) + 1.22874x10^(-3)* (Tf^(2))*(RH) + 8.5282x10^(-4)*(Tf)*(RH^(2)) - 1.99x10^(-6)*(Tf^(2))*(RH^(2))
Summer Simmer	SSI= 1.98(Tf - (0.55 - 0.0055(RH))(Tf-58)) - 56.83

Index(SSI) =	

Saturation Vapor Pressure(Mb)=	Es= $(6.11*10^{(7.5*Tc/(237.7+Tc))})$

Vapor Pressure(Mb)= From Dew Point	E= $(6.11*10^{(7.5*Tdc/(237.7+Tdc))})$

Vapor Pressure(Mb)= From Temp and Humidity	E = $(6.11*10^{(7.5*((Tc - (14.55 + 0.114 * Tc) * (1 - (0.01 * RH)) - ((2.5 + 0.007 * Tc) * (1 - (0.01 * RH))) ^ 3 - (15.9 + 0.117 * Tc) * (1 - (0.01 * RH)) ^ 14))/(237.7+((Tc - (14.55 + 0.114 * Tc) * (1 - (0.01 * RH)) - ((2.5 + 0.007 * Tc) * (1 - (0.01 * RH))) ^ 3 - (15.9 + 0.117 * Tc) * (1 - (0.01 * RH)) ^ 14)))))}$

Specific Humidity(kg/kg)=	SH= $(0.622*E)/(Mb-(0.378*E))$

Relative Humidity(%)=	RH= $(E/Es)*100$

Relative Humidity(%	RH = $(((6.11*10^{(7.5*((Tdf-32)/1.8)/(237.7+((Tdf-}$

) Knowing Tdf and Tf=	32)/1.8))))/((6.11*10^(7.5*((Tf-32)/1.8)/ (237.7+((Tf-32)/1.8)))))*100))

	Relative Humidity & Dew Point using Wet & Dry Bulb Temps
Relative Humidity and Dew Point knowing Wet & Dry Bulb Temps	'Saturation Vapor Pressure Wet $Ew = 6.1078 * exp([(9.5939 * Tw) - 307.004]/[(0.556 * Tw) + 219.522])$ 'Saturation Vapor Pressure Dry $Es = 6.1078 * exp([(9.5939 * Td) - 307.004]/[(0.556 * Td) + 219.522])$ $E = Ew - 0.35 * (Td - Tw)$ 'Actual Vapor Pressure Relative Humidity $RH = (E / Es) * 100$ Dew Point $Tp = -1 * \{[ln(E/6.1078) * 219.522] + 307.004\} / \{[ln(E/6.1078) * 0.556] - 9.59539\}$

Dew Point from just T and RH:	$Tdc = (Tc - (14.55 + 0.114 * Tc) * (1 - (0.01 * RH)) - ((2.5 + 0.007 * Tc) * (1 - (0.01 * RH))) ^ 3 - (15.9 + 0.117 * Tc) * (1 - (0.01 * RH)) ^ 14)$

LCL Height (Estimated	$H= 222(Tf-Tdf)$

[132]

FT)=	
LCL Height (Estimated Meters)=	H= 67(Tf-Tdf)
LCL Height in Millibars =	SP = (Surface Millibars) * 1000 ST = (Surface Temperature in ° C) + 273.16 SDP = (Surface Dew Point in ° C) + 273.16 'Find the LCL Level and Parcel Temp at LCL Height PT = ((1 / (1 / (SDP - 56) + Log(ST / SDP) / 800)) + 56) - 273.16 LCLMB = (SP * (((PT + 273.16) / ST) ^ (3.5))) / 1000
Rankine Temperature (R)=	R= Tf+460
Saturation Mixing Ratio(g/kg)=	Ms= ((Val(Humidity) / 100) / Val(MixingRatio)) * 100 OR MORE ACCURATELY 0.622 * Es/(P - Es)
Mixing Ratio(g/kg)=	M= RH*Ms/100 & M= ((0.622*E)/(Mb-E))*1000

Virtual Temperature(C)=	Tv= ((TemperatureC + 273.16) / (1 - 0.378 * (VaporPressure / StationPressure))) - 273.16
Lifted Index=	LI= Tc(500mb) - Tp(500mb)
Showalter Index=	SI= 1) From the 850mb temp, raise a parcel dry adiabatically to the mixing ratio line that passes through the Tdc(850mb) 2) From that point, raise the parcel moist adiabatically to 500mb. 3) SI= Tc(500mb) - Tp(500mb)
Vertical Totals =	VT= T(850mb) - T(500mb)
Cross Totals =	CT= Td(850mb) - T(500mb)
Total Totals=	TT= Tc(850mb) + Tdc(850mb) - 2*Tc(500mb)
(30 or greater strong	DCI= T(850 mb) + Td(850 mb) - LI(sfc-500 mb)

thunderstorms) Deep Convection Index =	
	KI= (T850 - T500) + Td850 - T dd700
K Index=	Basically double the KI value to calculate the chance of thunderstorms.
Energy Helicity Index =	EHI= (CAPE * Helicity) / 160000
Significant Tornado Parameter = F2+ damage associated with STP values >1	STP= (mean layer CAPE / 1000) * ((2000 - mean layer LCL meters) / 1500) * (0-1 km Helicity / 100) * (0-6 km Shear meters per second / 20)
ThetaE (any level) = [Saturated Potential Temperature]	ThetaE = (Tc + 273.15) * (1000 / Mb) ^ 0.286 + (3 * M) OR ThetaE = (273.15 + Tc) * (1000 / Mb) ^ 0.286 + (3 * (RH * (3.884266 * 10 ^ [(7.5 * Tc) / (237.7 + Tc)]) /100))

Theta (any level) = [Dry Potential Temperature]	Theta= $(T + 273.15) * (1000 / P) \wedge 0.2854$
WMAX (Maximum Potential Speed of an Updraft) =	WMAX = $((SQRT(2 * CAPE)) / 2) / 0.5148$
Vertical Velocities can overcome the cap if:	$VV > SQRT(2 * CINH)$
Convective Temperature=	CT = CCL Tc *(1000.0/CCL Mb)0.286 * (SFC Mb/1000.0)*0.286
Maximum Hail Size=	Hail = 2*((3*0.55*1.0033*(MVV*MVV))/(8*9.8*900))*100 MVV = Max Vertical Velocities in M/S
Normalized	NCAPE = CAPE / (ELm - LFCm)

CAPE=	<= 0.1 Weak Updrafts 0.1 - 0.3 Moderate Updrafts >= 0.3 Strong Updrafts

---

TQ Index (low top convection potential) =	(T850 + Td850) - 1.7 (T700) > 12 Storms Possible > 17 Low-Top Storms Possible

---

Delta Theta-E= (Wet Microburst Potential)	(SFCThetaE - LowestMidLevel ThetaE) >= 20 Wet Microbursts Likely <= 13 Wet Microbursts Unlikely

---

U and V Components of Horizontal Wind= SPD is in Knots DIR is in Degrees	$U = -(SPD * 0.5148) * \operatorname{Sin}(DIR * (PI / 180))$ $V = -(SPD * 0.5148) * \operatorname{Cos}(DIR * (PI / 180))$

Speed (Knots) and Direction (Degrees) from U and V Components	$Speed = \operatorname{Sqr}(U \char94 2 + V \char94 2) / 0.5148$ If V > 0 Then ANG = 180 If U < 0 And V < 0 Then ANG = 0 If U > 0 And V < 0 Then ANG = 360 $Direction = (180 / PI) * \operatorname{Atn}(U / V) +$

=	ANG

BRN Shear =	$0.5 \, ((\text{6km AVG U Component}) \wedge 2)$

Bulk Richardson Number =	BRN= (CAPE / BRN Shear)

Air Density (km/m3) =	D= (mb*100)/((Tc+273.16)*287)

Absolute Humidity =	Ah= ((6.11*10.0**(7.5*Tdc/(237.7+Tdc)))*100)/((Tc+273.16)*461.5)

Station Pressure =	Ps = Altimeter in Inches * ((288 - 0.0065 * Elevation in Meters)/288)^5.2561

Altimeter Setting =	As = (Station Pressure in MB - 0.3) * (1 + (((1013.25^0.190284 * 0.0065)/288) * (Elevation in Meters/(Station Pressure in MB - 0.3)^0.190284)))^(1/0.190287)

Pressure	Ap = (1-(Station Pressure in

Altitude   MB/1013.25)^0.190284)*145366.45
(Ft) =

    Be advised that this listing has been
compiled through various learning sources
and is accurate and up to date with current
meteorology methods. They are advanced for
a lot of amateur weather enthusiasts;
however, learning these equations can speed
along your learning process in the field.

Special Thanks

I would like to take this opportunity to personally thank a few people and organizations who have believed in my work and helped me get through all the tough feedback from amateurs and professionals alike in the weather community. Without these people I would be lost today.

Erika Martin - This wonderful meteorologist from the channel 8 WTNH news in Connecticut helped foster my desire to pursue weather as more than just a hobby, and aspire to go beyond the criticism of a few lost souls. Her help and support helped me follow my work and dreams. Thank you Erika!

Randi Chenkin - Randi has been an influential member to me and has supported me through all of the tough times I have had on this journey through meteorology. Her work has been in emergency radio and fighting childhood obesity, and her Randirobics program has been a huge help in providing the guidance and help parents need to point their children into the right direction of a healthy lifestyle. Without her kind words of encouragement, I would still be struggling to find my place in the community. Follow her on twitter @Randirobics !

SHTFLI.Com - These guys have been a huge help in raising awareness and emergency preparations on Long Island and into New England. The work and commitment these people provide in their services to the people of Long island is an invaluable service, and they help fuel my passion for using weather to help people. Your work and dedication has not been in vain, and I look for these providers of emergency radio to flourish over the next year or so! Follow them on twitter @SHTFLI !

I would also love to thank all of my adoring fans in both the Facebook and twitter worlds who have given me nothing but positive feedback on my hard work and dedication to the world of weather. Without you I would not be able to see the results of my work in action, and I would not know when I have made a mistake. I will continue to foster the friendships and communications from all of you, and will continue to help others in the ways that you have all helped me! Thank you!

I would also like to thank my father, may he rest in peace. You showed me that the world will not stop and wait for me to get on board. Reality is harsh sometimes, and you served as the basis to show me that sometimes life is way too short to hold back what you are capable of. Sometimes the world tries to hold you down, and in order to rise above it you need to make the first move. When we lost you, no amount of reassurance or promises to myself could ever replace what you meant and still mean to me. I love you dad, and always will. Thank you for everything you taught me about being a man and chasing your dreams.

I would also like to thank my mother for helping me critique this book. Without her poking and prodding me on each and every little thing, this book may not have been as informative as it is. She believes in giving the customer a quality product that they can go back to again and again without getting bored or tired of it. Because of her, I continued to work hard in research and compile together the best data possible for all of you.

Resources and Contacts

The National Weather Service: www.Weather.Gov
National Hurricane Center: http://nhc.noaa.gov
Storm Prediction Center: http://spc.noaa.gov
Wxedge CT - http://www.wxedge.com
Weather-Talk - http://www.Weather-Talk.Net
GFS Website: www.ncdc.noaa.gov
ECMWF Website: http://www.ecmwf.int

Nick Szankovics Twitter: @weather_talk
Erika Martin Twitter: @erikamartin
SHTFLI twitter: @SHTFLI
Rick Knabb, NHC Director: @nhc_director
Storm Prediction Center: @SPC
National Hurricane Center: @NHC

Direct any questions or comments to
webmaster@weather-talk.net or @weather_talk.